NOT WITH OUR DAUGHTERS

BOKO HARAM & THE KIDNAP-
PING OF 300 NIGERIAN
SCHOOLGIRLS:

A NEW PATTERN OF TERROR

THE WORLD MUST UNITE AND

STOP.

Richard Simons, Ph.D.

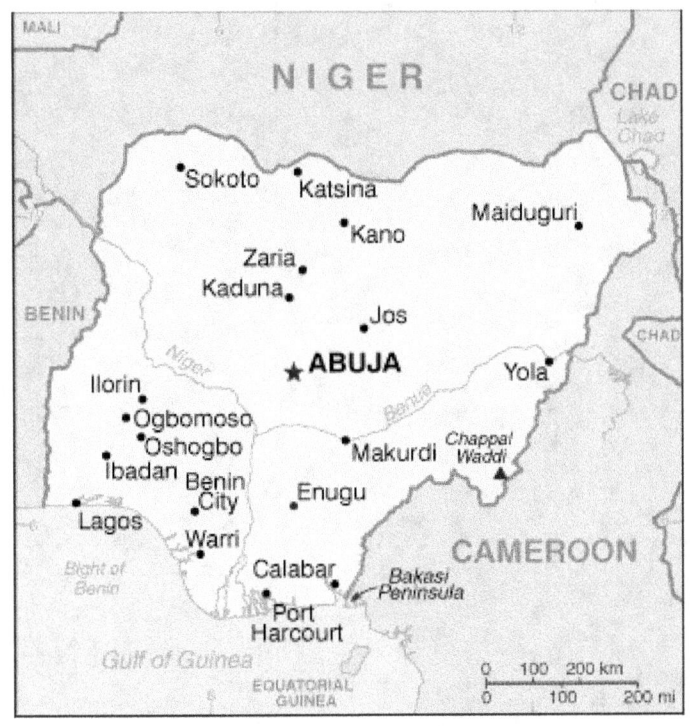

Source: World FactBook 2014, Washington, DC.

To all people affected by terrorism - victims of terrorists and their families across the globe.

"It is a heart-breaking situation, outrageous situation…All along, we have imagining what could have happened to our daughters."[1]
  - President Barack Obama.

"Our prayers are with the missing Nigerian girls and their families.[2] - First Lady Michele Obama.

Boko Haram is not just an act of terrorism. It is a massive human trafficking moment and grotesque.[3]
  - Secretary of State, Senator John Kerry.

"My birthday wish this year (2014) is.to see Chibok Schoolgirls returning to their homes"[4]
- Malala Yousafzai, Taliban shooting victim and Paki stani education activist.

Prologue

PROLOGUE

APRIL

It is an atrocious, despicable and outrageous act with impunity against humanity. The world woke up on April 14, 2014 with the breaking news that more than 300 schools girls were abducted from their dormitory at the Government Secondary School, Chibok, Maiduguri in Northern Nigeria. The news shocked the world with widespread international condemnation of the terror tactic. Nigeria's dreaded terrorist group Boko Haram claimed responsibility for the kidnapping.[1] About 53 of the girls escaped from the terrorists, leaving 276 teenage girls between the ages of 12 and 16 still missing and under their abductors.

One year after the abduction of the Chibok schoolgirls, the students are yet to be rescued. Rather, incidents of young girls (some as young as 10 years old) are used by Boko Haram as suicide bombers, making people wonder whether the adducted school girls are sent on suicide missions against their will. This is particularly worrisome as most of the incidents of detonated bombs were discovered strapped on the bodies of these young girls and were remotely-controlled.

On March 12, 2015, Boko Haram pledged allegiance to Islamic State in Syria (ISIS); which was immediately accepted by Islamic State (IS) in Syria and Iraq. This was happening as President of Nigeria, Dr. Goodluck Jonathan in an interview with the *Voice of America*, confirmed an intelligence report that revealed Boko Haram fighters have traveled to the Middle East for training with Islamic State (IS) militants.[2]

Boko Haram's name is derived from Hausa language, spoken in Maiduguri where the Jihadists' headquarters is located. It means, "Western education is sin." Information provided by the Christian Association of Nigeria (CAN) revealed that more than 165 of the abducted schoolgirls were Christians.[3]

Not With Our Daughters – Boko Haram & the Kidnapping of Nigerian Schoolgirls: A New Pattern of Terror the World Must Unite and Stop was motivated by the unprecedented incident of kidnaping of schoolgirls from Chibok and the reactions by the international community to the cruel and horrendous act of using our most precious gift to the society - our daughters to terrorize us. Writing this book, the author adds his voice to the international campaign to rescue kidnapped schoolgirls and end terrorism. The objective of writing the book is also to highlight Boko Haram's assaults, suicide bombings, tortures and kidnapping that revealed how deadly the terrorists are – looking back to its origin and the deadly assaults on the public, government security agencies and foreign workers.

Ever since Boko Haram started its deadly assaults on foreign workers, Nigerians, the military, police and other security agents, it has left more than 13, 000 people dead (some sources estimate the number of people massacred by Boko Haram Jihadists at 15, 000). On June 25, 2014 Nigeria was playing Argentina in the World Cup in Brazil, Boko Haram detonated bombs loaded into cars that were parked at very popular Abuja shopping complex, Banex Plaza killing ten people. Just as the emergency crews were to rescue the wounded, another bomb blast went off killing more people at Emel plaza, a very crowded & busy business center at the heart of the Federal Capital city of Abuja. All these incidents took place in spite of the presence of U.S., British, French, Chinese, Canadian, Israeli, Iranian technical and military experts on the ground in Nigeria to assist in the rescue efforts of the kidnaped schoolgirls. In fact, Boko Haram remains irrepressible as evidence in this book showed a spike in military-styled assaults and suicide bombing by the terror group.

From the time when Chibok schoolgirls were abducted, Boko Haram has killed more than 1000 Nigerians comprising civilians, military and, police officers and secret agents. When more than 1000 Nigerians killed since April 14, 2014 is compared to about 12, 000 killed since 2009 when Boko Haram started its bloodbath on the population, the number is no doubt staggering and disturbing. Some of the military officers have been killed while were ambushed as they were on convoy to smoke out the terrorists from the large and tropical Sambisa forest, which the group has used as their base.

Similarly, prominent members of the society in Maiduguri were ambushed, kidnapped or killed. The Emir of Gwoza, Alhaji Idrissa Shehu Timta was a victim of Boko Haram terrorism. The terrorists murdered Idrissa Shehu Timta when the convoy of cars Shehu Timta was traveling with other two Emirs, the Emir of Uba, Alhaji Ali Ibn Ismaila Mamza II and the Emir of Askira, Alhaji Abdullahi Ibn Muhammadu Askirama was attacked. Ismaila Manza II and Mohammadu Askirama were abducted.[4] There was no information about the whereabout of the abducted Emirs. It was however learned that the abducted traditional and religious rulers were whisked away to the notorious Sambisa forest where the 276 abducted Chibok schoolgirls are supposedly held. This incident took place on Biu-Garkida highway in Maiduguri. Garkida is a border town with Adamawa state, and 241 kilometers south of Maiduguri, the Bornu state capital.

Also in Chibok, very close to Government Secondary School compound where the schoolgirls were abducted, Boko Haram conducted another kidnapping - this time the terrorists took away 35 school girls on May 29, 2014 to Simbisa forest. On June 8, 2014, Boko Haram abducted another set of girls, this time their target was ethnic Fulani women. This happened after the assailants attacked a settlement known as *Garkin Fulani* at midday Sunday, and ordered the women into their vehicles at gunpoint. The number of girls kidnapped by Boko Haram since April 14, 2014 abduction of almost 300 school girls is estimated at 100. It was gathered that the last batch of kidnapped schoolgirls was among the 65 girls that escaped from Boko Haram as the military attacked one of the terrorists' forest bases on July 6, 2014.[5]

This manuscript was in progress, but the event of April 14, 2014 - the abduction of more than 300 Nigeria schoolgirls from Government Secondary School, Chibok, Maiduguri facilitated its completion and release. The schoolgirls were kidnapped from their school compound as they gathered to take their West African Examination Council (WAEC, equivalent of SAT in the USA or GCE in the United Kingdom).

However, the reality that Boko Haram has adopted this new pattern of kidnapping – teenage girls (for that matter) as part of its tactic of terror to inflict more injuries – including emotional wounds compelled the change of title for this book. The goal is also to highlight the outrageous and heartbreaking situation and examine what the global community could do to stop kidnapping of anybody, not to mention girls, even after Chibok schoolgirls are rescued, as the long battle to stop terrorism is ongoing. Boko Haram has links to Al-Qaeda, al-Qaeda in the Islamic Maghreb (AQIM), Al-Qaeda in the

Arabian Peninsula and al-Shabaab.[6] Therefore, a global coalition force is needed (which has started with Britain, the United States, Canada, France, China, Israel and Iran technical and security experts in Nigeria at the press time to assist the country rescue the kidnapped girls). However, it is the intention of the author to inform that Boko Haram is not just a Nigerian problem. It is a global problem of huge costs and implications. Terrorism from West Africa's front needs a long-term and sustained military and intelligence collaboration with the Nigerian government. The kidnapping of the Chibok schoolgirls granted an opportunity to tackle the global terrorism that has infiltrated not just Nigeria neighboring countries of Cameroon, and Chad, but extending across the African continent as witnessed in Chad, Mali, Algeria and Libya.

Before April 14, 2014, Boko Haram terrorists have attacked Nigerians (Christians and Muslims), Churches, Mosques, and institutions of government. It has taken its serial assaults to market arenas, shopping centers, recreational parks, motor parks, security posts, military barracks, airports and rural villages. Boko Haram has also taken its campaign to Islamize Nigeria to the capital city of Abuja - including attack on the United Nations headquarters. Boko Haram has also for the first time in its history of its deadly military-styled assaults, suicide bombing and kidnapping attacked Lagos. On June 25, 2014 suicide bombing attacks, four people were killed when a female suicide bomber detonated a bomb vest loaded with explosives.

Boko Haram's erratic leader, Abubakar Shekau claimed the two attacks in Lagos. He made the claim in an AFP (French News Agency-obtained) video released on July 14, 2014 through social media. Shekau mocked the #BringBackOurGirls campaign. In the broadcast purportedly marking the 3-month anniversary since Chibok schoolgirls were kidnapped, Shekau remarked the girls would not be freed until the government released the "army" of Boko Haram fighters held in Nigeria jails.[7]

Overall, Boko Haram has rendered the Northern and Central Nigeria unsafe and vulnerable to violence. There are security alerts across Nigeria's West and Southeast regions - that the Jihadists may be sending mercenaries to these parts of the country, thus the decision by the governments in Lagos and Port Harcourt to round up suspected unemployed youth roaming the streets in these states.

Nigeria is therefore a nation on the global spotlight, as Boko Haram draws on the media attention on Nigeria and intensifies its military-style assults. This is happening even as the global community mobilizes to search for and rescue the abducted schoolgirls. For the fact that Boko Haram has killed more than 1000 people since it kidnapped the Chibok schools girls on two incidents – one on April 14, 2014 and another on May 29, 2014 tell about the bestiality of this group. Al-Qaeda even condemned its tactics and seemingly, senseless cruelty and capricious violence against civilians.[8] Pundits have described Boko Haram as more dangerous than Al-Qaeda.

Boko Haram's 'quick–wittedness explains how the terrorists were able to invade a school and kidnapped more than 300 students in a state that has state of emergency imposed on the region; coupled with mixed reports that there were presence of village vigilante and military patrol along the roads leading to Chibok and across the state of Maiduguri. The state of emergency notwithstanding, the police and vigilante groups from another account were not present when the schoolgirls were kidnapped – raised questions whether there was an inside informers that allowed Boko Haram easy pass to the school premises.

Many questions were asked and they remained unanswered about how the terrorists were able to pull through their tactics manipulating their way and avoided being caught by joint security operatives in Chibok town that included the police, the military and State Security Services. The question about how the Jihadists drove 7 to 10 truckloads of schoolgirls out from Chibok into Sambisa forest without any challenge from the security agents or the villagers were also among unanswered questions Across Africa communities, including Chibok town, the collectivistic culture and the value system – provide that neighbors watch over their neighbors and property. Therefore, it became incomprehensible that such a convoy of men riding in trucks and motorcycles could easily escape with the number of kidnapped girls after hours of operation, and the military or the police were not alerted.

Security experts knowledgeable about terrorists and kidnappers disclosed that it was very suspicious that nobody responded to rescue the girls. In essence, the whole saga revealed either collaboration or an inside job. As pundits also disclosed, it may also be the terrorists were masters in their new tactic of kidnapping such a large number of people …. that it developed a very strong surveillance and built a strong monitoring and security walls to avoid being caught in the act of abducting 300 school girls.

Some experts disclosed that for the abduction to be successful, it means Boko Haram kidnappers must have used both psychological and their military expertise to successfully accomplish their goal. In essence, it must have taken craft - dangerous one for Boko Haram to pull through this tactic. Others believed that there might be inside informers that enabled Boko Haram succeed in executing their scheme, since there was no response from the police or the military throughout the duration of the abduction incident. The number of people kidnapped in one incident was unprecedented in Nigeria, thus making the beastly act one of the dreadful terror acts to be pulled through by any kidnappers.

They were still unanswered questions on the whole Boko Haram's abduction of Chibok schoolgirls – what happened before and after the abduction of the schoolgirls. The questions are many but nobody is providing adequate answers. In the absence of satisfying answers to what actually happened (including whether the girls were actually kidnapped or a political ploy), conspiracy theories continue to arise, occupying the empty spaces of unanswered questions.

Some of the conspiracies about Boko Haram have persisted even before the kidnapping of the Chibok schoolgirls. However, the answers that this book provides are not about conspiracy theories. They are based on empirical evidence, news media reports and eyewitness accounts. The author also informs readers about some of the underlying political wrangling within the ruling party and opposition party in Nigeria that emboldens Boko Haram.

Unfortunately, the unsettling political wrangling and the disagreements between the ruling and the opposition political parties in Nigeria fuel the conspiracy theories. The political environment similarly provides the reason why there has not been a common front or determination to mobilize a united force to address the problem posed by Boko Haram. Amidst the unsettling wrangling and playing party politics, the author warns that for the international community and their tasks to be successful, the rivalries US – China, US-France the U.S. and Iran, and Iran-Israel must be left behind. Since, it may difficult to leave these differences in politics and policies behind, it is no wonder that some Nigerians are concerned whether the mission by these nations to send technical and security experts to assist Nigeria rescue the Chibok missing girls and also fight Boko Haram would ever be successful.

Some Nigerians are already worried with the "invasion" of countries to assist Nigeria. Some critics describe their coming to Nigeria as "another invasion for partitioning of Africa." All the same, other opinions reveal that it does not matter whether the nations are in Nigeria for their own benefit as long as the situation does not continue to deteriorate. Nevertheless, the critical question remains unanswered, and it will always be. Will politics between United States, China, Iran and Israel make the purpose of these nations coming into Nigeria to rescue the Chibok girls impossible?

Nigeria has since assumed command and control. She has enabled all the countries volunteering to the rescue mission of Chibok schoolgirls sign an undertaking in the name of memorandum of understanding. However, it remained to be seen how Nigeria would be able to lead, manage and implement decisions when the United States and its allies are in charge of the drones for the operation and coordinating both the tactical, military and psychological strategies to persuade the terrorists release the abducted teenage school girls.

While nations volunteering to the mission to rescue Chibok school girls may not agree on most matters – religion, fundamentalism, human rights, freedom fighters, and even who is a terrorist and who is not, it is no wonder some Nigerians are wondering whether the mission to rescue the abducted schoolgirls and fight terrorism will be successful or the politics between these nations play to distract them from the mission. The author therefore recommends that precautionary measures be taken, and activities of the technical and security experts limited to the rescue mission or else, their involvement in Nigeria's internal affairs – politics in particular may see these nations wanting to assist Nigeria get tangled in domestic politics and not accomplish the goal of rescuing the girls. Thus, they may frustrate rather than motivate or improve the fight against terrorism from that part of the world. [It is regrettably as envisaged that the international coalition to rescue the schoolgirls could not hold. United States it was gathered pulled off from the arrangement].

Boko Haram had previously attacked several schools, boys were their victims. Their lives were not spared - their throats were slit with machetes, but girls have been released in those attacks. Why did the abductors of Chibok schoolgirls pretended to be "saving" the girls only to load them into trucks and drove into the forest with their captors? Previously, Boko Haram had invaded schools and asked girls in the schools they have attacked to go home, get married or convert to Islam.

Unknown is whether this pattern of abducting schools girls is a new playbook by Boko Haram or a pattern that Nigeria is being used as a testing ground for future terror tactic by Al-Quaeda, since Boko Haram has affiliations and shared terror tactics and financial resources with Al-Qaeda in the Islamic Maghreb (AQIM), Al-Qaeda in the Arabian Peninsula and Al-Shabaab. It is no wonder that the world is outraged by this incident. The abduction of girls – a majority of who are Christians speaks volumes of a bigger problem, a complete lack of impunity by terrorists to pull yet another tactic, to commit this kind of crime and get away with it. The abduction of the schoolgirls is not only disturbing, but it tells the world that the war on terror is not yet over.

The world should also realize that Boko Haram was formed in 2002 when Miss World was about to take place in Nigeria. Though the group never assumed the name Boko Haram, the terrorist opposition to beauty pageant was synonymous with the opposition of Boko Haram to education. While the mob that stopped Miss World pageant taking place in Nigeria because hosting the Miss World – the beauty pageant was 'public exposure' of naked women and a form of "Western hedonism" that must be stopped. In 2002, the extremists mobilized, rioted and forced Miss World pageant out of Nigeria. Miss World Pageant took place in London after 200 lives were lost.

The reality of the kidnapping of more than 300 schools girls from Government Secondary School Chibok is that (if nothing is done) the global community will be signaling to terrorists and to Boko Haram in particular our lack of determination to bring back our daughters and fight terrorism. Any lack of serious action to rescue our daughters, the world will be setting a wrong precedent of do-nothing. Our inaction will motivate terrorists (not just Boko Haram) to hurt and hunt us. It is the anticipation that by the time this book is gone to press or published, the girls will be rescued. Even after the girls are released, the war on terror is not yet over. It is a war against terror that is ongoing against insurgents working hard to bring down the government and introduce their ideological sharia laws. Nigeria government is already away of these goals.

Therefore, the united front to bring back the girls is what is right (and the world is already doing) in joining Nigeria's effort to fight Boko Haram and stop terrorism. If the world does nothing (I reiterate and emphasize) the possibility that Boko Haram with its affiliate will be motivated to pull this through elsewhere in the world is possible. As Al-Qaeda is known to pull intrigues and repeat test runs, they have tested elsewhere. It is a pattern of terror that is likely to repeat elsewhere eventually. It may also not be surprising if Boko Haram or its affiliates pull the tactic through elsewhere in Africa, Middle East or around the world before this book is published. Therefore, if the adoption of Chibok schoolgirls was a litmus test by Al-Qaeda to be executed by Boko Haram, the world must unite to stop this tactic.

Ultimately, the world seems to be uniting – as evidence of support from the international community reveals a united force against Boko Haram and terrorism. The responses have been encouraging, especially from the United States, France, Britain, Canada, China and Israel. Iran also joined in the campaign – a positive development from the country's leadership that some Nigerians are questioning. The support is a boost to the fight against Boko Haram and the mission to rescue the Chibok schoolgirls. It is global effort to assert pressure on Boko Haram to release kidnapped Chibok schoolgirls and the renewed fight against terrorism that motivated the #BringBackOurGirls' campaign must continue until this goal is achieved.

The Nigeria government as pundits pointed out should have come up with this request for international assistance long time ago since Boko Haram started its assaults, suicide bombings, and kidnapping in 2009. However, a majority of the people agreed that this is not the time for criticism, whether it is the Nigeria military or President Goodluck Jonathan, and his government of how they have handled the kidnapped Chibok schoolgirls. It is rather time to put in place and execute whatever military and intelligence plans are necessary to rescue the kidnapped girls without the distraction of politics. In essence, Nigerians and the global community must come together in the fight to rescue the Chibok schoolgirls and fight terrorism.

This book as earlier revealed was in progress before the kidnapping of 300 Nigerian schoolgirls at Chibok. However, it offers at a glance perspectives about why Boko Haram continues to wax stronger and has increased its frequency of operation (and with impunity) even with presence if international rescue mission in Nigeria. With Boko Haram allegiance to Islamic State in Syria in March 2015, the groups outreach and support becomes more worrisome.

The book also examines the history and the origin Boko Haram, who finances the organization, why the terror group targets Christians, and Muslims who opposed their Jihadists' ideology? Why politics in Nigeria between the North (Muslims) & South (Christian) frustrates policies to arrest the situation in the North and North Central parts of Nigeria. Politics in Nigeria and the manner it is played is frustrating federal government effort to take firm position that would have eliminated Boko Haram.

Several questions are asked, why is the Nigerian army unable to stop Boko Haram? The reasons are many including that war on terrorism is not won by how equipped the army is – else the war on terror in Afghanistan and Iraq would have been won very long time ago. It is also not about lack of equipment or training to fight Boko Haram. It is also not about morale of the army. It has more to do with all these inferences than the politics on the ground among opposition and the ruling party in Nigeria.

Nigeria has offered military support to United Nations Peace Mission and on its own liberated Liberia, Sierra Leone; why it seems Nigeria is now incapable of tackling terrorists that is home grown but with support from internal financiers and external groups such as Al-Qaeda, Al-Shabaab, Al-Qaeda in the Arabian Peninsula and al Qaeda in the Islamic Maghreb (AQIM) beats imagination? There is no doubt that the Nigerian military had proven records of its worth in the civil war, the liberation of Liberia and Sierra-Leone; serious wars and in the process returned democracy to those countries, but fighting terrorism - as even superpowers have realized, is more than using armored tanks, grenade and bombs to flush out and terminate the terrorists.

Fighting terrorists is like any guerilla warfare within residential populated areas, they could easily fight their targets and infiltrate into the population and use people as human shields. In essence, fighting terrorists like Boko Haram fighters needs human intelligence more than war bombs, mortars and rocket grenades to win the war. Terrorists, like gorilla militia could fight and easily infiltrate into the population, making it difficult for the insurgents to be tracked and eliminated.

There are however, some crucial and unanswered questions about Boko Haram. There is claim that the Bornu state government under the All Progressive Congress Party (APC) is using the instability and Boko Haram uncontrolled attacks to embarrass and unseat president, Goodluck Jonathan who is considering running for reelection in 2015. There is also the allegation and suspicion from the ruling party, the People's Democratic Party (PDP) that the relationships between Boko Haram and politicians in Maiduguri and the entire Northern and Central Nigeria is the reason the insurgents operate freely, sometimes beating intelligence leading to operation failures by the joint military force set up to dislodge the terrorist group.

The sources of information to Boko Haram fighters to avert joint military forces from crushing the terrorists, and who provides insurgents the intelligence regarding military operations remains unknown. It is uncertain to determine whether the statement by President Goodluck Jonathan that some sympathizers of Boko Haram are within his administration did affect the morale of brigade commanders. For instance, why coordinated efforts by the authorities to fight Boko Haram seemed un-coordinated, the question- is there insubordination in the military and the police, thus giving Boko Haram the edge in the war against terrorism? Military convoy of soldiers going after the terrorists in the week preceding the kidnapping of the Chibok schoolgirls was ambushed. The military, it was gathered sustained heavy casualties in the ambush.

Meanwhile, Boko Haram attacks have huge impact on the relationship between Muslims in the North and Christians in the South. While Nigerians on individual levels do work together at government and business sectors, but on politics and religious matters, they cannot compromise or remain as a cohesive group to resolve matters affecting overall relationships among ethnic groups.

The book also examines the introduction of sharia laws in 14 of the 36 states - how the sharia emboldens extremists, and impact relationships among more than 250 ethnic groups in Nigeria. While the perception is that these sharia laws embolden the extremists, but among the decent, moderate and peaceful Moslems in Nigeria, they are stunned by activities of some amidst them that use the same religion to carry out violence against others. Islam, among these moderate Muslims is a religion of people and sharia never encouraged suicide bombings, attacking Christians in their places of worship even on holy days such as Christmas and Easter. Now with 276 Chibok schoolgirls (180 of them are Christians) still held by their captives; the world is ready to assist Nigeria rescue the girls and on the front in this battle against terrorism from this part of the world.

While the global community reacted to Boko Haram's horrendous act of kidnaping Chibok schoolgirls, the bigger question is at what point will the engagement of Britain (former colonial authority in

Nigeria), United States, Britain, Canada, France, China, Israel and Iran be successful without these countries meddling into Nigeria's politics.

In fact, some of these countries are suspects by Nigerians of having ulterior motives for coming to Nigeria other than to rescue the Chibok schoolgirls. While there is evidence to support such claims, Nigerians are worried that events in the Middle East with Israel and Iran may at some point play on the ground in Nigeria as these nations do not see eye to an eye on the problem they have volunteered to assist resolve. In addition, United States, China, Britain, France are suspicious of each another. This question becomes more difficult to address whether these nations will focus on mission of the schoolgirls or will politics that divide them including ways and means of fighting terrorism prevent them from achieving the task the world has placed hope that the abducted schoolgirls will be rescued.   The other key question is for how long will it take the coalition to find and rescue the schoolgirls? Will the search and rescue drag on? This is because terrorism is a long-term cancerous tumor that never and will never go away.

However, it is anticipated that the campaign to stop Boko Haram fighters like the war on terrorism in Afghanistan and Iraq should be sustained over a long period. What nations participating in the rescue mission must do is to focus on their mission without involving in the muddy waters of politics in Nigeria. Evidence showed that more than 1,500 people were killed between the months of January and March 2014; this was before more than 300 girls were abducted (of which 53 escaped).

More than 1000 Nigerians have been killed since the international community mobilized to rescue kidnapped Chibok schoolgirls. The statistics points to the enormity of the problem. It is very unfortunate that the global response was slow, but never late, since the invasion and abduction of Chibok girls brought world attention to Boko Haram that has killed more than 12, 000 Nigerians and foreigners since 2009 when the Jihadists began their bloody assaults on innocent Nigerians and foreign workers in the country.

Another evidence of Boko Haram's bestiality was revealed as the global community was expressing outrage over the abduction of 276 schools girls; and few days after, the terrorists invaded another village in neighboring Nigeria - Cameroon border town, and sacked families from their homes. As if the terror was not enough, Boko Haram insurgents invaded market place, and at the end killed more than 150 people because, the terrorists perceived that the villagers were not collaborating with their demand of using their village for settlement.

Boko Haram fighters were also suspecting the villagers for giving information to the authorities about their (Boko Haram's fighters) whereabouts. Eyewitness account disclosed that joint military force and intelligence team were using the village as their base, while authorities intensified efforts to flush out Boko Haram from Sambisa forest. Sambisa forest is a huge tropical forest stretching as far as villages in Borno state to border villages located in Chad and Cameroon. The impacts of terrorism and sectarian violence have effects on Nigeria's economy. This is even as Nigeria showed a strong economic growth of 7 percent Gross Domestic Product (GDP) according to IMF and World Bank Report.[9] Pundits believed Nigeria economy would have showed more growth has the violence in the North and Central Nigeria be curtailed.

Nigeria is strategically located - political and economic powerhouse to Africa, and the global village. It is therefore important that the assistance - military and intelligence being provided by nations that volunteered in the Chibok schoolgirls rescue mission must see their presence as a long term investment to bring stability to the region and the rest of the world. The assistance should be more than training, military, intelligence, but financial support; else, Boko Haram with its financing from internal and external sources will have advantage over the Nigeria military and police whose budgets are inadequate to wage a long term war against terrorism. In essence, investment to fight the war on terrorism from Nigeria front must be genuine, sustainable over a long period. If it is not, the decision to assist Nigeria and stop the threat posed to Boko Haram may be a futile endeavor.

Will foreign assistance to fight Boko Haram avoid the failed status pundits have predicted of Nigeria? The answer is yes and no. However, the presence of International community in Nigeria to stop the terrorists will distract Boko Haram for the mean time from pursuing its agenda of a failed Nigeria State. As witnessed in Afghanistan, Iraq, Somalia, Libya, Mali, Tunisia, Algeria, Egypt, any break in the fight against terror is taken advantage, and further empowers the terrorists in their fight against the state and authorities. How resolved these countries assisting Nigeria to rescue the abducted schoolgirls are without mingling into Nigeria politics as 2015 presidential election draws close in Nigeria will also determine if Nigeria will be a stable or unstable nation after the presidential election.

The Joint Military Task Force appointed by President Goodluck Jonathan has achieved tremendous results in killing some of Boko Haram's leaders (some Nigerians may disagree), but the war is not over until the snake – Boko Haram is terminated from its head. That head includes investigation and probably arrest of some Nigerian politicians, identifying the external sources allegedly supporting, and financing Boko Haram.

Boko Haram has financiers such as Al-Qaeda in the Arab Peninsula, Al-Qaeda in the Mediterranean and Al-Shabaab in Somalia and some Nigerian politicians. The terror groups (Al-Qaeda and Al-Shabaab) have enormous wealth and network that must be dislodged or terminated for Nigeria and the world to be secured. With Boko Haram allegiance to ISIS, the matter is altogether a different challenge to the global community. This is the reason opinions to the question whether Nigeria will succeed as one of the most prosperous economies in the world in the 21st century as predicted by IMF and World Bank will depend on Nigeria's leadership and Nigerians alone.

In essence, international assistance to rescue the Chibok schoolgirls must be part of the long-term plan by the global community to fight terrorism from Africa's front. The success of the fight to get rid of Boko Haram and end terrorism, therefore, will be determined by leadership Nigeria leaders provide, and the efforts by all Nigerians to be vigilant of their environment while assisting the authorities with providing information that could lead to foiling attacks before they take place. The global community to stop Boko Haram agenda of a failed Nigeria state may be successful, but it must not only be sustained through military campaign alone.

While some Nigerians frowned at the presence of international military and intelligence experts in the country, describing their presence as another form of an open door to 'imperialism' or the scrabble for Nigeria's oil, a majority of Nigerians believed that the assistance of the global community to fight Boko Haram was long overdue. President Jonathan, they said should have sought the help of international community long ago in his administration's policy to fight the insurgents.

Some Nigerians interviewed remarked that they do not mind any name the presence of international experts is called, as long as Boko Haram's threats to peace and stability of Nigeria are stopped. As one commentator explained, "It is not about oil or invasion now. When Boko Haram kidnapped our daughters, they have overstepped the boundaries. Nigerian children are like our daughters, I am an American.... and no matter where you are and where you come from, once you attack our helpless daughters, we must fight to rescue them." A Nigerian, who asked for anonymity also remarked, "Whether it was President Goodluck Jonathan who invited the international community or even you.... does not matter anymore. Let the international community do their job and let us see those who are behind Boko haram."

Meanwhile, the First Lady of the United States, Michelle Obama joined the campaign to rescue the abducted Schoolgirls at Chibok, on the eve of Mothers' Day celebration in the US in 2014. She described as "unconscionable act" the kidnapping of the schoolgirls and terrorists attempt to stop them from getting education. The first lady who took over the president's weekly radio and Internet address, remarked that as millions of people around the world, President Barack Obama and herself were "outraged and heartbroken" over the April 14 abduction of the girls from their dormitory. She disclosed,

> "In these girls, Barack and I see our own daughters," (referring to Malia, 15, and Sasha, 12). "We see their hopes, their dreams and we can only imagine the anguish their parents are feeling right now." [10]

First Lady remarked that what happened in Nigeria is not an isolated incident, but is a story we see every day as girls around the world risk their lives to pursue their ambitions.[11]

Not just from the White House, but across the globe, people are more motivated after the April 14, 2014 kidnapping of Chibok schoolgirls to fight Boko Haram, and terrorism. Evidence shows that there is no going back even after more than 365 days and the girls are yet be found or rescued. This commitment is one that the global community must not allow to subside even after the girls are eventually rescued. Nigeria is Africa's political and economic heartbeats and allowing it collapse is a risk that world cannot afford at this time, in particular the Europeans and the United States. In today's global village where nations and people are interconnected, distance is no longer a problem to what world citizens can do; the same also applies to what enemies could do distance notwithstanding. When the global community are terrorized and afraid, the terrorists take advantage of our fears to hurt more – they toast, boast, and likely to repeat the same behavior when we do nothing. When we are emboldened, just as the global community is about finding Chibok kidnapped schoolgirls (and even when they are eventually rescued); we have decided that terrorists will never win, rather we are ready to pursue them to their caves and forests, and terminate them as they are nuisance to the society.

CHAPTER 1

Boko Haram – Why New Tactics of Kidnapping Chibok Schoolgirls?

More than 365 days has passed, and the kidnapped Chibok schoolgirls are yet to be rescued. The fears of the global community have increased as news from Nigeria reveals of a spike in the number of young female suicide bombers that Boko Haram sends on suicide missions. It was revealed from the attacks by these young suicide bombers in Kano, Abuja, Bauchi and Lagos, that they were driven to their targets, and their abductors used remote-controlled device to detonate improvised bombs padded on the girls' vests.

Boko Haram going this far after the April 14, 2014 kidnapping of the Chibok school girls revealed an unstoppable acts of cruelty and human bestiality. Though the Nigeria government has ruled out that the teenage girls sent on suicide missions by Boko Haram were the Chibok schoolgirls; however, the use of young female suicide bombers – some as young as 10 years old raises more fears to what next the Jihadists are up to. When it is recalled that young girls, the same group of people the Jihadists do not want to gain education or participate in beauty pageants are the ones they sent on suicide mission, it is hard to imagine what is in the minds of the Jihadists. It is no wonder that it is becoming every day more serious and complicated in interpreting what next these terrorists are up to. Boko Haram's allegiance and acceptance of the allegiance by ISIS in March 2015 worsen the fears of the global community and the call for international coalition to combat the terrorist group.

When Boko Haram invaded Government Secondary School, Chibok and kidnapped teenage girls, the incident shocked the world with international condemnation of the terror tactic. The world was still pondering the reasons why Boko Haram decided to pull this serious act of emotional attack and trauma to parents of abducted Chibok schoolgirls, Nigerians and the global community. With more girls (some as young as 10 years old) sent on suicide missions than before the kidnapping of the Chibok schoolgirls, the interpretation of what next in terms of Boko Haram's rashness and brutality becomes more difficult to tell.

Nevertheless, several thoughts have begun to emerge from reasoning as experts piece together theoretical evidence and ideologies of these Jihadists as expressed in their playbook. Trying to piece the minds of kidnappers and terrorists together is not easy, and offer explanations why they act the way they do has become even more overwhelming. It may seem unconscionable that a group of men drove into Chibok village where teenagers were taking their exams and at the early morning hours whisked them away against their will. The explanation why this happened and what interpretations that may be attributed to the behavior remains a mystery.

However, drawing from the perspectives of French philosopher, Michel Foucault, the question his theoretical evidence provides could illustrate the reasons for Boko Harams actions – the quest for power control and intimidation. Foucault's perspective provides a narrow window to explain what may be in the minds of terrorists. Foucault asked "Are prohibition, censorship, and denial truly the forms through which power is exercised in a general way, if not in every society? Most certainly, as in "the battle of all battles" – often using women's bodies to engage in battles.[1] Boko Haram's kidnapping of innocent girls between the ages of 12 and 16 as victims of their battle (terrorism) situates the discourse about their ideology, the battle to Islamize Nigeria and their use of the abduction as power to terrorize people. The terrorists also uses their kidnapping of teenage daughters for their publicity and as "subjects" for barter in exchange for Boko Haram members held in prisons by the authorities in Nigeria. As witnessed with all "wars", women are often drawn into them – whether as sexual objects to be raped, trafficked, converted into wives or used as slave laborers.

Boko Haram as witnessed with YouTube video released where Boko Haram's leader Abubakar Shekau was acting erratic; he was laughing and cajoling and boasting his readiness to sell our girls into slavery. Shekau was taunting his "power" of exploitation (of women), using the teenagers vulnerability and their sexuality to exercise power while promoting their (Jihadists) ideology. Boko Haram Jihadists are exploiting on earth (rather than in paradise) the paradox of capturing virgins as an ideological ascension to heaven and killing infidels who dare challenge his group. It is the same power Jihadists express that killing infidels is justified by their religion. No doubt, Boko Haram terrorists are also using our daughters to extend their 'mentality of brutality.'

Watching the videos on YouTube, the images of Boko Haram leader Abubakar Shekau – laughing bragging, cajoling, and seemingly unperturbed, makes the public wonder what mental torture these teenage girls are going through in the hands of Jihadists whose value is using deadly force to achieve compliance. The evidence that majority of the girls kidnapped are Christians creates the tremendous fears of what next would happen at the hands of extremists whose ideology as expressed by Shekau is exploitative of women. No doubt, the girls are under gripping fears of being raped, assaulted, and even killed. As already revealed, all the 165 Christians among the kidnapped girls have been forced to change their religion. As the world witnessed on the video, the kidnapped girls on hijabs and reciting verses from Koran said it all. Similarly, evidence of spikes in the number of teenagers sent on suicide bombing missions in the months of July and August 2014, barely more than 365 days after Chibok schoolgirls were kidnapped raises the fears that some the abducted girls may be dispatched against their wishes as suicide bombers.

Abubakar Shekau's narratives about selling "your daughters into slavery.....as he pointed out, there is market for selling girls." [2] His statement painted a picture of how far the Jihadists could go with their beastly acts. His statement also reveals rhetoric about 'power,' a battle of control, repression, and domination by invoking issues about women's sexuality and their bodies through mediated forms. By mediated discourse.......Boko Haram is using the image of a drunken, drugged, and rambling leader, Abubakar Shekau as he boasts to the world about kidnapping "your" girls and use them for whatever purpose that suits the Jihadists.

Shekau bluntly threatened to use the kidnapped teenagers for whatever purpose he desires including selling schoolgirls into slavery. "Allah, he says I should sell. He commands me to sell, "[3] Boko Haram leader Shekau boasted. These statements show the mind-set of terrorists. They are always happy when we are terrorized. Terrorists enjoy the physical and psychological tortures of their victims, pattern of assault the World must fight to stop.

Whether society calls Abubakar Shekau's cajoling ignorance -

but like any terrorists, he craves free publicity. In spite of ideologies being submerged in ignorance, Boko Haram fighters seem to be getting too much of publicity even at the pains of parents and outraged global community. However, Boko Haram's tactic of abducting Chibok schoolgirls to terrorize people could also be explained from the Foucault perspectives on *The History of Sexuality*, control, knowledge, and power.[4] Shekau's act boils down to use of "fear" factor as instrument of terror to achieving their objectives.

It is yet to be determined whether the kidnapping of our daughters is terrorists' ploy to gain attention or hold them as ransom for money, but the international community must stop this exercise of power madness. Former Nigeria's president Olusegun Obasanjo in an interview with Hausa Service of the British Broadcasting Corporation (BBC) remarked that some of the kidnapped girls might be released, some of the girls will be pregnant. He disclosed that Boko Haram fighters may at a stage be finding it difficult to cater for the babies in the forest and may set the baby and mother free. President Obasanjo, who revealed that he has contacts with the Jihadists also revealed in an interview with the radio station expressed his fears that "some of the kidnapped girls might never return again."[5] 365 days have passed and the girls are yet to be rescued.

Foucault's theses did address the relationship between power and knowledge (*The Archaeology of Knowledge*), and how it is used as a form of social control through societal institutions. His thought has been highly influential in both academic and activist groups. Apparently, Boko Haram may have realized that knowledge is power and stopping women gaining education is empowerment of women that must be stopped.

Terrorists are borrowing and applying the wrong side of Foucault's philosophy, just as they are using their own version of the Koran for their selfish goals and at the same time smearing Islam as a peaceful religion of more than a billion people around the world. Foucault went on to publish *The Archaeology of Knowledge, Discipline, Punishment, and The History of Sexuality*. In these theses, he developed archaeological and genealogical methods that explained the role power plays in the evolution of discourse in society.

Boko Haram's ideology denies women education. The Jihadists denies women their fundamental human rights and their rights to empowerment and contribute to the socio-economic development of the society. For the 300 kidnapped Chibok schoolgirls, denying them education is in part denying the girls power (education and what long-term huge benefits education brings to the girls and the society). Recall the cliché, when a mother gives birth to a woman, she gives birth to a nation (of people). Moreover, when she delivers a boy, she have given birth to just an individual.

Education and empowerment of women is a non-ideological and non-negotiable matter. It is an indispensable human rights issue about women and children in any society that wants to advance beyond Stone Age. There is no place in ideology or politics to deny women education.

However, to Boko Haram ideologists, education and empowerment of women are evil and must be stopped by all means possible. Shekau's mockery of women as he was laughing and boasting on camera as he mocked about his "treasures" and selling the women into slavery as if they were his property. He was shamelessly informing the world that he is in charge – a false sense of reality, but to him "power."

Boko Haram is also adopting the humiliation of 'your" women

rhetoric to intimidate and terrorize the people while playing their politics with terror along religious lines– since the majority of the kidnaped girls are Christians. The terrorists goes further, using psychological mind-control to torture their victims, the parents and families of abducted schoolgirls and the concerned members of the global community. It is for these reasons that global community must unite and not allow Boko Haram succeed in its mission to terrorize us further. The terrorists are testing our patience and reaction to their tactic of abducting our teenage daughters from their classrooms, stop them by force from gaining education because according to the Jihadists' ideology "Western education is evil" and must be stopped. Their action, they perceive and believe in it that it is part of their agenda to Islamize Nigeria by taking Nigerian women out of their classrooms by force.

Boko Haram's messages and using the media as propaganda tool is to show their relevance while at the same time prolonging the discourse on terrorism. They have used suicide bombings, military assaults, and these tactics were not enough; now kidnapping of teenage daughters as emotional trauma and a test-run to check our commitment to fight back. Any parent with a daughter between the ages of 12 to 16 knows too well about the bond between father, mother and daughter, and for that to be taken away in a split of a second and by force could be traumatizing.

In essence, it appears Boko Haram is advancing its warfare tactics to another level - physical, psychological and emotional assaults of the highest order ever witnessed in the history of terrorism. At the same time, the Jihadists are exerting more fears on their victims and parents by controlling and using our children – girls for that matter through violation of their spaces, their bodies, their religious beliefs and controlling where they would be located through captivity whether it is in Sambisa forest or elsewhere in Nigeria, Chad or Cameroon. Most of the girls kidnapped were supposedly virgins (12 and 16 years of age). Their abductors knew about their ages (ages that daughters are in their primes and very close to their parents – fathers in particular). It is the most enduring moments that fathers have very strong family ties and connection of true love and attachment to their daughters. Terrorists exploited those connections to hurt parents and the rest of humanity.

Boko Haram is also exploiting Chibok schoolgirls' private spaces, so they invaded their dormitory at early morning hours and took the teenage girls away in a place parents considered as secured as their homes. Boko Haram sustains their ever-growing hate for Western education, which it considered a sin by making sure that these girls are prevented or stopped from gaining knowledge. Knowledge according to Foucault is power.

However, the motives driving Jihadists' ideologies and reality of what the group's goals are remain very confusing. In essence, it is not yet clear what their motives are for kidnapping the girls apart from their claims that they wanted to exchange the abducted schoolgirls with Boko Haram prisons identified by Abubakar Shekau as his "soldiers' captured and detained by federal authorities. However, investigation revealed that Jihadists use kidnapping and extortion as sources for funding their terror activities.

Boko Haram has never asked for ransom other than exchange of prisoners with the girls. However, men including teenage male students (another set was kidnapped in August 2014 and held hostage as this book was about going to press). These male students, it was gathered were forcefully recruited into their fold. That is after the Jihadists have brainwashed or administered drugs on them or enticed the conscripted to be fighters for the Boko Haram causes.

Until the April 14, 2014 Chibok schoolgirls kidnapping, Boko Haram rarely abduct women (not to mention girls), and if they do, one of the most dominant reasons is that girls are kidnapped to be used as human shields against retaliatory attacks. The Jihadists' ideology used to be the spiritual beliefs that when they kill infidels, they gain their rewards from Allah. Their rewards include houses in paradise, and sleeping with beautiful virgins as brides. Similarly, when they are killed by any means for upholding their ideologies, they believed they would immediately go directly to paradise as martyrs. In that make-believe paradise, they will be greeted at the door of 'heaven' with virgins as their wives – which means that death is the beginning of their pleasure and a new life.

Boko Haram as witnessed from the kidnapping of Chibok girls seemed to acting against their so-called… declared ideology. The belief of being ushered into "heaven" to marry and sleep with "virgins" after they were dead or killed as a result of holding to their ideology. As a critic described Boko Haram's beliefs, their ideology is a charade and a distraction. He expressed, "these sadists by kidnapping teenage schoolgirls from Chibok are no longer waiting to reap their so-called 'reward' in paradise. They want to kidnap teenage girls, molest them on earth rather than waiting for the virgins to be offered to them in their so-called paradise."

Jihadists also believed when a community is attacked, the people are forced to mourn as the world is doing now with the kidnapping of Chibok schoolgirls. When Jihadists attack a community or gathering of people, [and they succeed], they also believed those of them killed during the battle will go to paradise. This means that they have assisted the enemies to go to hell – meaning any infidel killed will go to hell. They see such infidels as deserving the death, and they (Jihadists) have no regrets for such deaths. In essence, killing an infidel is perceived as rites of passage to paradise. These testaments from scholars in Islamic and Jihadists studies may be illogical, and strange, but these beliefs are real as manifested by actions of Jihadists in the society they live. Since these thoughts are embedded in Jihadists' mindsets, there is no conviction otherwise against these beliefs. Similarly, there is not much anybody outside their group could do to educate them that their beliefs are wrong especially when they are driven by kidnapping, suicide bombing and military-style attacks on civilian population.

Sometimes, when Jihadists abduct women, they are used as domestic servants. In other circumstance, the fundamentalists would force the abducted women to marry them. There is also the belief that women having children for Jihadists would permit them have direct descendants or protégé that will inherit their struggles, while sustaining their battle perceived as a long-term goal for the terrorists. There is no doubt in their mind set that children born directly by the terrorists will sustain the chain of terror after they may have passed on.

Terrorists as witnessed in Afghanistan, Iraq, Al-Qaeda in the Mediterranean, and Al-Shabaab in Somalia crave attention and media publicity. Boko Haram has exemplified the same pattern of a publicity–hungry attitude. The have skills and expertise on the use of the social media – Facebook and You-Tube in disseminating their messages of terror. They are using these social media for their global outreach than any menacing group has ever in the history of the Internet and terrorism. Boko Haram's kidnapping of teenagers at Chibok Girls Secondary School Maiduguri has brought world's attention to the terrorists and their beastly act. However, at the same time Boko Haram enjoys the global publicity, even though the international community still has the advantage of using the same social media to mobilize, rally around Nigeria, as a motivation to rescuing our daughters and fighting terrorism.

It is yet to be known whether the abduction of Nigerian schoolgirls is one-time incident, but like Al-Qaeda, of which Boko Haram is affiliated; the terrorists never failed to pull through their tactics and often repeat the pattern of violence elsewhere. It is their tactic – Al-Qaeda hallmark and now Islamic State of Iraq and Syria (ISIS) On August 16, 2014, Amnesty International disclosed that Jihadists have kidnapped more than 3,000 women and girls in a 2-week rampage. Amnesty International said the victims, some just babies, were snatched from villages overrun by the heavily armed jihadists. According to the report, the abducted women face the prospect of being forced into marriage or sold as sex slaves.[6]

Whether Nigeria was being used as a testing ground to challenge global will power, and determination to either stop or continue to tolerate the pattern of outrageous kidnapping of people; the Islamic State of Iraq and Syria (ISIS) have since Boko Haram incident took place-kidnapped women mainly from minority tribes of the Kurds and Yazidi sects. The ISIS fighters – known for torture, public punishments and executions of those opposing them – have gained significant ground in both Syria and Iraq after its initial assault on the city of Mosul in mid-June. The group has since declared the creation of an Islamic State, or caliphate, straddling the Iraq-Syria border. [7] This is even as

Al-Qaeda did kidnap students – mainly boys from their school bus in Iraq on June 25, 2014 as they were driving to take their exam.[8]

This incident occurred in less than two months after Boko Haram outrageous act of kidnapping Chibok schoolgirls. These abductions of 300 Chibok schoolgirls and the same pattern of adducting teenagers, women and children are great concern to the global community and requires attention stop this tactic immediately, or the Jihadists will be emboldened by our inaction.

The fundamentalist in Nigeria, for example, aborted the Miss World pageant, killed 200 people and the government of Nigeria, like the rest of the world, was silent. Boko Haram uses big events to gain attention and pull-through its assaults, suicide bombings or kidnapping to gain attention and drive up their recruits. With these ploys and crave for attention, in addition to the pains these terrorists sustain on their targets and humanity, by not doing anything, we are opening ourselves up for more attacks.

Boko Haram, founded in 2002 when Miss World was about to take place in Nigeria. Fundamentalists now known to be some members of the terrorist group did succeed in stopping the event holding in Nigeria because they were against women's public exposure or nudity – a form of Western hedonism that must be stopped. Through 'rioting," fundamentalists orchestrated violence that stopped the Miss World pageant from taking place. The so-called "rioters," now identified as likely members of Boko Haram Jihadists attacked and killing 200 Nigerians.

It would therefore be a grave mistake to allow Boko Haram kidnap our daughters and walk away free. In the words of Nobel Prize Winner and a Nigeria literary giant, professor Wole Soyinka, "There have been numerous incidents like this," he told Christine Amanpour of CNN; the 2011 Boko Haram bombing of a United Nations compound in Abuja and extremists' unrest over a 2002 beauty pageant being just two examples." [9]

CHAPTER 2

Not With Our Daughters – Boko Haram & the Kidnapping of 300 Nigerian Schoolgirls: A Pattern of Terror the World Must Unite & Stop.

Boko Haram has been a ticking time bomb waiting for time (since 2002 when it was founded) to explode. Maybe the Nigerian government under-rated the capabilities of the terrorist group until April 14, 2014 when its members invaded Government Secondary School, Chibok in Maiduguri and abducted 300 Nigerian school girls. About 53 escaped from their kidnappers. The schoolgirls were between the ages of 16 and 18 years old.

However, before this incident, the estimate of Nigerians and foreign workers killed by Boko Haram was about 12,000. The figure according to Human Rights Watch was an under-estimation of the actual casualties of Boko Haram assaults. This statistics was an estimate because some of the terrorists' attacks were not reported. However, evidence showed that between January and February 2014, Boko Haram killed more than 1,500 Nigerians; most of their victims had their throats slit with machetes with some of gory images posted on their website and played on video in social media. After April 14, Boko Haram has killed more than 1000 people and the list continued to rise; thus some sources have put the number of people killed by Boko Haram at 15,000.

Nevertheless, before these incidents, in 2009 - two weeks before Boko Haram's declaration of 'Jihad' to Islamize Nigeria - the

British intelligence report warned of the extremists' looming terror attacks. Boko Haram's threat must be watched since according to Algerian Secret service, el-Khabar (known to have the biggest intelligence gathering on Al-Qaeda and al Qaeda in the Islamic Maghreb (AQIM), the terrorist group has links with al Qaeda in the Islamic Maghreb (AQIM). AQIM has its North African headquarters in Algeria." [1] Boko Haram was also said to have received training in Algeria.

In 2010, the Algerian government provided Nigeria intelligence reports confirming that Boko Haram has links with al Quida in the Islamic Maghreb (AQIM). Algerian authorities warned of threats posed by the group that Nigeria must be on alert. With all the intelligence to Nigeria authority, it confirmed as security sources revealed that a previously unknown group (Boko Haram) has received training and support from al Qaeda.[2]

Africa Command (AFRICOM) Commander General Carter F. Ham in September 2011 also confirmed that Boko Haram along with other African and global terror groups were targeting Westerners and specifically the U.S. Since Boko Haram is considered a major political threat to Nigeria, he warned that the synchronization of their efforts entailed raising funds across international boundaries to achieve their goals. While Boko Haram's funding is local, General Ham warned, Boko Haram seemingly enjoyed the same international support from the United Kingdom and Saudi Arabia.

"Replacing the Afghanistan' situation in Nigeria entailed funding floating across the world including some Islamic organizations such as Al Muntada Trust Fund with headquarters in the United Kingdom and the Islamic World Society with headquarters in Saudi Arabia."[3]

The Algerian Deputy Foreign Minister, Abdelkader Messahel, confirmed to journalists from intelligence report that revealed Boko Haram and Al-Qaeda have been collaborating and coordinating their activities "We have no doubts that coordination exists between Boko Haram and al Qaeda." Reuters news agency quoted Messahel, "The way both groups operate and intelligence reports show that there is co-operation".[4] AQIM grew out "of the conflict in Algeria between the government and Islamist militants". The intelligence report disclosed, "In the past few years, it has expanded its activities to include Mali, Niger and Mauritania but was not thought to have reached as far south as Nigeria"[5]

Nigeria's former Chief of Army Staff (COAS) Lt General Azubuike Ihejirika told reporters in an interview that the Army recognized the involvement of foreigners in the operation of Boko Haram. He disclosed that weapons and other sophisticated military ammunitions captured from the group established foreign backers to the group. "The types of weapons we have captured, the type of communication equipment, and the expertise Boko Haram has displayed in the preparation of improvised explosives devices...these are pointers to the fact that there is international involvement in the terrorism going on in Nigeria."[6]

With Boko Haram, having all these links with Al-Qaeda, al Qaeda in the Islamic Maghreb (AQIM), and Al-Shabaab, and with their alliance to Islamic State militants in Syria, there is no doubt that Boko Haram is a threat to the world - not just Nigeria. With thousands killed from military-style assaults, bombings and kidnappings by Boko Haram and the attempt by the Jihadists to stop Westernization of Nigeria, there seemed to be no end in sight to their attacks

The Jihadists' attacks have spread to the Federal Capital Territory, Abuja, but also to Jos and in the last days of June 2014 attacked Bauchi State (Middle Belt). With the international team of tactical and security experts on the ground in Nigeria, Boko Haram is moving their war beyond just the North and Northeast to other parts of Nigeria.

Boko Haram's name is derived from Hausa language spoken in Maiduguri where the group's headquarters is located. Boko Haram has utilized suicide bombers to attack Christian churches consecutively in 2011 and 2012 during Christmas and Easter eve holy masses. Mosques were attacked, where clerics that opposed Boko Haram ideology were hacked to death in their places of worship. Hundreds were killed. The terrorist group has attacked police stations, military barracks, joint police and military checkpoints, as well as military bases. In each of these incidents, Boko Haram engaged in serious confrontation with the security agents.   In some scenarios, the terrorists overpowered security agents on duty by their numbers and superior firepower. One of such scenes was the August 26, 2014 media report that Boko Haram fighters disarmed 480 Nigerian soldiers and the soldiers defected to Cameroon to avoid fighting Boko Haram. The Director of Defense Information, Major-Gen. Chris Olukolade, in a statement on the alleged disarming of the 480 soldiers in Cameroon, said: "The Nigerian troops that were found in Cameroon was as a result of a sustained battle between the troops and the terrorists around the borders with Cameroon, which saw the Nigerian troops charging through the borders in a tactical manoeuver…….Eventually, they found themselves on Cameroonian soil. Being allies, the normal protocol of managing such incident demanded that the troops submit their weapons in order to assure the friendly country that they were not on a hostile mission." [7]

Boko Haram has also attacked places like beer parlors and motor parks mainly used by Southerners – a majority of whom are Christians. Boko Haram targeted luxury buses at Sabon Gari motor park loading passengers – the transportation hub for Igbos. The victims in the attack as expected were mainly Christians of Igbo extractions travelling to the Eastern part of the country. More than 100 people were killed in that particular attack.[8] The terrorists have also attacked the United Nations building for second time at the Federal Capital Abuja. They attacked a transit hub (station) in the month of April, about 10 miles to the capital city, Abuja where people converge to board their daily buses to work and businesses. Boko Haram's military-style, suicide bombings, and invasion of institutions considered as embracing Western values such as the invasion of high schools in the Yobe, the execution of the male students and other kidnappings are inhuman acts and serious threat to Nigeria's internal security.

On April 14, 2014, that pattern changed when a group suspected to be Boko Haram in its usual military-style assaults, invaded Government Girls Secondary School in Chibok, Bornu State and kidnapped more than 300 schoolgirls; a number that came down to 276 after some of the students escaped and got back to Chibok. Police sources disclosed that the actual number abducted by Islamic extremists on April 14, 2014 was more than 300.[9] The kidnapping that took place early morning hours in Chibok went unchallenged as security guarding the school were over-powered by the number of terrorists with what some witnessed described as more high-powered guns and ammunitions than any military could possess. The attack of the Government Girls School, Chibok came barely hours after explosives had killed and wounded more than 75 people, about 16 kilometers from the capital city of Abuja.

Boko Haram never pulled this pattern of kidnapping of teenagers or any group as large as Chibok schoolgirls since 2009 when the group launched its first militant assaults in Nigeria. Since their targets were women and young girls on that April 14, 2014 incident in Chibok, Boko Haram successful tactics sent a chilling message of the group's character and inhuman behavior. Boko Haram's dexterity also revealed how a public place for education and knowledge enrichment is turned into threatened and defenseless conflicting space for our daughters. This situation could explain why the world is shocked and are asking questions - where is our daughters? And the hashtag [#] BringBackOurGirls emerged as campaign slogan to rescue the Chibok schoolgirls

All these incidents were taking place as people around the world woke up and suddenly witnessed the pro-democracy uprising and the death of 100 pro-democracy members in Kiev, Ukraine. The media attention that focused on Ukraine and the Missing MH 370 Malaysian flight changed immediately when Nigeria's war on terror that has gone unnoticed since 2009 suddenly became the headline news with the kidnapping of the Chibok schoolgirls. It may be an understatement to infer that it was not until April 14, 2014, that Boko Haram began to attract attention despite the earlier warnings as revealed earlier that came from Algerian, European and USA African Command intelligence. As a concerned Nigerian Ms. Ann Henshaw put it, "It seems that Nigerians are numbed that they do not care anymore. She went on to say, "200 of our girls are missing and government in Nigeria and the people across the world are doing nothing – something is wrong here."

Although the media could do much at a time – meaning what stories they could cover at a particular situation and timeline, some individuals and organizations using social media moved ahead and mobilized the audience. Change.org, for example, mobilized the global community through social media to act. The social campaign slogan 'Free Our Girls' also galvanized the global community and the media to pay attention to the cause of the organization to free the 276 abducted Nigerian schoolgirls still missing.[10] Alexis Okeowo, *The New Yorker* writer, who has followed the story of the abducted girls, remarked that anyone can actively help in this situation by merely giving the story the exposure it deserved.[11]

While the parents of the kidnapped girls were not satisfied with the updates from the government, news reports claimed that the abducted girls have been whisked across Cameroonian border towns into Chad and Cameroon. Other sources revealed that the girls were being sold into slavery – some forced into marriage with Boko Haram members and others as brides to militants at about 2,000 naira — $12 per girl. "I abducted your girls; I will sell them in the market, by Allah. I will sell them and marry them off; there is a market for selling humans. Women are slaves. I want to reassure my Muslim brothers that Allah says slaves are permitted in Islam,"[12] Abubakar Shekau, Boko Haram leader threatened.

On April 30, thousands of people, including some parents of the kidnapped and still missing girls, stormed the National Assembly in Abuja, asking the government about the whereabouts of their daughters. They insisted that the government provide them answers. Some parents said that they were ready to go across the borders in Cameroon and Chad, even at the risk of their lives to ensure they rescue their missing daughters from the terrorists.

These abduction scenarios demonstrate how dangerous Boko Haram terrorists are, and the situations further paint gory images of the brutality of the Jihadists, how they shift their patterns of operation all geared to terrorize people. With their pattern of attacks, whether by Al-Qaeda in Afghanistan or in Iraq, Al-Shabaab in Somalia and in Kenya, not only do these terrorist groups do collaborate in the areas of logistics, but also in training in military tactics and financial resources. However, the pattern of kidnaping schoolgirls is a new tactic that the world must unite and stop. This is a clarion call to world leaders for action against terrorists and attention to what is happening not just in Nigeria but also in Iraq and Syria. Jihadists from more than 50 countries have been identified in the Jihadists fights in Iraq and Syria. Boko Haram affiliation with the Jihadists around the world with resources that include oil wealth is impending danger that the world must watch with every interest and determination to act before it is too late.

Boko Haram, according to sources, received most of its arms from Libya.[13] The Malian-Jihadists attempted to oust a democratically elected government is a tip on the iceberg of what Al-Qaeda and Al-Shabaab supported terrorists can do. The Jihadists in Mali took over the democratically elected government, and it took France intervention for the insurgents to be defeated. The Malian government was restored, as the Jihadists fled to neighboring West Africa countries including Nigeria.

On June 3, 2013 - US offered rewards for capture of African militants after the group was declared a terrorist group. About $27 million was offered for information leading to capture of African terrorist leaders. The highest reward of up to $7m is for information leading to the location of Boko Haram leader Abubakar Shekau. Smaller rewards were offered for leading figures in Al-Qaeda in the Islamic Maghreb (AQIM) and the Movement for Unity and Jihad in West Africa. A reward of up to $5m was offered for veteran militant Mokhtar Belmokhtar. His *Blood Battalion* was held responsible for an attack on a gas plant in southeast Algeria in January 2013 in which at least 37 hostages, including three US citizens, were killed.[14]

Boko Haram with its unstoppable attacks on Nigeria and its second attack in Abuja in May 2014 showed that it would take the global community's resolve and determination to reduce the strength of Boko Haram's insurgents. The terrorists' attacks on Nigeria could be seen along the pattern of extremists fighting the state as witnessed in Afghanistan, Iraq, Egypt, Somalia, Libya and now Syria.

Boko Haram killed more than 1,500 people between February and March 2014.[15] In Adamawa, Yobe and Borno, the centers of Boko Haram's attacks, more than 70 percent of the people live on less than a dollar a day compared to 27 percent in Lagos and about 35 per cent in the Niger Delta. 85 public schools in Borno were closed because of the insurgence.[16] In the week of March 24, 2014, more than 125,000 students in Maiduguri no longer attend classes because of violence and insecurity in the state. According to Kashim Shettima, governor of Borno state, the Islamists burned more than 500 blocks of classrooms in 2013 alone, some more than twice.[17] After the schools have been rebuilt, they are facing an enormous enemy that needs coalition forces to tackle, not by the state alone.

Nigeria is Africa's most viable economy. It has abundant human and natural resources, economic and political powers as well. Allowing Nigeria to be degraded or be a failed state is a black eye to the world. As former Ghanaian President, Jerry Rawlings painted the pic ture of Nigeria's Boko Haram, "The thing should not be left for government alone, but the society must begin to examine itself, come together, strategize together; otherwise, ladies and gentlemen, it may not be able to handle this problem today or tomorrow," he asserted. [18] He continued, "Nigeria's political might is about 35 per cent in Africa and that is why Nigeria must show the way in leading Africa. The way the world is going, Nigeria must not suffer vulnerability, or others will take advantage of the problem."[19]

Femi Kayode, an outspoken politician and former Minister of Aviation, remarked that the agenda of Boko Haram and those that are behind it, both locally and their international backers, is not limited to northern Nigeria, and neither has it ever been. He said Boko Haram's goal is to conquer the whole country and establish their own caliphate.

> "They wish to impose their strange values and barbaric be
> liefs on the rest of us by force. There are some leaders in
> Nigeria, backed by Al Qaeda, the Taliban, al-Shabaab and
> emboldened by Arab money and salifist philosophies that
> honestly believe that if Nigeria is not ruled by a northern
> Muslim, then there must be no peace or there must be no
> Nigeria at all."[20]

Kayode continued, "Whether we like to admit it or not, this is the bitter truth. As far as Boko Haram is concerned, it would be better to establish a pre-historic Islamic fundamentalist state, like the old Taliban-controlled Afghanistan, where full Sharia law is practiced and where Boko Haram leads and holds sway, than to have a modern-day secularist Nigerian state where a southern or northern Christian or a moderate Muslim rules."[21] This situation is becoming daring as Government of neighboring   country,   Cameroon,   alerted   the   Nigerian   gov ernment that some Nigerian Muslim clerics living in the border towns of Cameroon and Nigeria are recruiting Boko Haram members in their mosques." [22]

As already witnessed with Al-Qaeda in Afghanistan and in Iraq, when pressures from security agents are on the group, they often devise new tactics and often pulled through to hurt physically and emotionally, further terrorizing humanity. Similarly, as witnessed in Nigeria with the raid at the Government College, Yobe (Boys College) at the same time the Al-Shabaab attacked Westgate Mall in Kenya in September 2013 that left more than 60 people dead and more than 170 wounded. The attacks seemed coordinated, successfully executed deadly assaults pulled through in two countries at the same time – similar to Al-Qaeda patterns of attacks in Africa and elsewhere in the Middle East.

On August 7, 1998, two massive bombs exploded outside of the U.S. embassies in Dar es Salaam, Tanzania, and Nairobi, Kenya, killing 224 and injuring 5,000.[23] Before the incident, nothing was then known about the terrorists or the group responsible for these attacks. With Nigeria and Kenya events happening simultaneously and more evidence of coordinated attacks – sometimes signifying collaborations (the hallmark of Al-Qaeda), it is no wonder that the global community must unite, not just to fight terrorism, but terminate Boko Haram; otherwise, there may be long-term consequences. The pattern of deadly attacks and mass killings as the world is already witnessing with threats to global peace, security, and stability by Jihadists in Iraq and Syria and Nigeria cannot be taken for granted.

CHAPTER 3

Boko Haram – In the Beginning

The fundamentalist group, the *Jama'atu Ahlis Sunna Lidda'awati Wal Jihad*, is also known as Boko Haram. The group name, Boko Haram in Hausa language spoken in Maiduguri, the enclave the group uses as its headquarters. It translates into English meaning "Western education is sin."

The fundamentalists' group was declared a terrorist organization in Nigeria in 2002 because of its affiliations with other Islamic groups such as the Al Qaida in Islamic Maghreb (AQIM) and the Middle East. Boko Haram's goals set to Islamize Nigeria (by using North and North-Central Nigeria as its testing grounds) and to eventually make all states in the federation administered under extreme forms of sharia laws. In essence, it has its goal of not just Islamizing Nigeria, but pursuing the goal to make Nigeria a failed State, Boko Haram envisages that Nigeria will be a 'failed' state; therefore, it hopes to use the country as a base to extend its Jihad to Western targets in Europe and the United States.

Boko Haram's history dated back to Muslim fundamentalism era in the 80's in Nigeria. Since 2009, it has metamorphosed into an independent, but extremely violent Jihadist group. The group's emergence into the national limelight in Nigeria was in 2009, when Boko Haram's leader, Mohammed Yusuf was killed while in detention by Nigerian security forces after a sectarian violence that left more than 200 people including Boko Haram Jihadists dead. Since then, the group has expanded its terror attacks to targets in the North and the North Central parts of the Nigeria, to the Presidential Lodge known as *Aso Rock* in Abuja and into other enclaves originally thought to be safe.

First, Boko Haram started focusing its attacks on the military and on government targets. Not long after, it shifted to targeting Christians and Christian Churches mainly where Igbos of Southeastern Nigeria worshipped. Boko Haram dispatched suicide bombers and cars loaded with explosives into these places of worship including on Christmas and Easter mass celebration.

Boko Haram has extended further its attacks to gathering spaces of Igbos in the Sabon Gari, Kano. Beer parlors and entertainment centers where Igbos come together for social and entertainment activities were not spared. Transport hub where the Igbos boarded buses transporting their citizens from Kano to Eastern part of the country were also targeted. Thousands have died in these attacks. Boko Haram has also attacked schools in the North, invaded students' dormitories, dragged them out at very early morning hours, and ordered students to identify themselves by their names. Students with names that sounded Christian were singled out, blindfolded and taken away. Students who identified themselves as Christians were eventually beheaded with machetes or execution style on the streets. Jihadists see the students and people attacked as "infidel's representing corrupt Western influence.

Muslim leaders who also criticized or were against the group's ideology and did so publicity were targeted and killed. As at December 2013, Boko Haram has increasingly turned its weapons on civilians particularly after locally-formed vigilante groups were out to protect their villages and towns from the insurgents. Some of the villagers acted as mercenaries by providing information to the Joint Military Task

Force set up by President Jonathan about the whereabouts and activities of the terrorists. Since Boko Haram acted like gorillas (they attack and fade into the local population), when they wanted. This has posed the greatest challenges to the joint military and police agents going after the terrorists. Their guerilla tactics have been daunting for the security agents that struggle to avoid high civilian casualties as Boko Haram members are known to fade into the population after their attacks.

Boko Haram terrorists have also raided and burnt down several villages whose members of the community refused to accommodate the fighters. The terrorist have sent many residents into the streets as refugees – that is if the villagers made it alive. Sources at the displacement villages disclosed that thousands of villagers had fled and lived on top of hills; they have vacated their homes – if the houses were not razed down; they were taken over and occupied by Boko Haram fighters. The terrorists have not relented in their fight to take over villages in Maiduguri, even with the presence of the international team to assist Nigeria rescue the kidnapped Chibok schoolgirls, the fighters have proved difficult to track and be contained.

Nigeria's federal authorities had initially thought that Boko Haram was an insurgent it could manage on its own without foreign assistance. However, that oversight has been a mistake that the government acknowledged when it finally invited international community for assistance after the Chibok schoolgirls were kidnapped. In retrospect, the British Intelligence reported two weeks before Boko Haram's outright declaration of 'Jihad' in Nigeria in 2009 that an Al-Qaeda-type of group had plans to use Nigeria as a base toward launching attacks on European cities and the United States. The group's threats according to Algerian Secret Service, el-Khabar included using their affiliation with

Al-Qaida to engage in the kidnapping of Westerners across the Sahel region comprising Senegal, Mauritania, Mali, Burkina Faso, Niger, Nigeria, Chad, Ethiopia and Eritrea.[1] From these senseless killing of innocent Nigerians and foreign workers in Nigeria, the group has since showed no restraints even at the time this manuscript was going to press in August 2014. Boko Haram has repeatedly attacked civilians' targets, police, military installations – including the destruction of public and private properties have not stopped. One of its victories in August 2014 was the overrun of a battalion of 500 Nigerian soldiers by Boko Haram fighters. Cameroon Army spokesman, Lt. Col. Didier Badjek said the soldiers had been disarmed and were being accommodated in schools in Cameroon. Boko Haram on Sunday, August 24, 2014 released a video in which it said it had established an Islamic state in the towns and villages it controls in the northeast especially Gwoza. The Nigerian soldiers are in the Cameroonian town of Maroua, about 80km (50 miles) from the Nigerian border, Lt. Col. Badjek told the BBC.[2]

With unending incidents of deadly attacks, it therefore remains to be witnessed how Boko Haram with its affiliations to Al-Qaeda networks in the Middle East, the Mediterranean, and East Africa would ever be dismantled. President Goodluck Jonathan revealed during a conference hosted by French president Francois Hollande in France to address Boko Haram terrorism in Nigeria, and the abduction of 300 Chibok schoolgirls that Boko Haram has killed more than 12,000 Nigerians and foreigners since 2009.[3] Among its victims were mothers, children and fathers. Among them more than 100 passengers killed by a suicide bomber in a parking lot at Sabon Gari, in Kano States known to be a hub of Igbo's from Christian South. The incident occurred a week after the group posted on its website the execution of construction workers it kidnapped with seven other foreigners.

Among foreigners killed were British, Italian, Spanish, and Lebanese. The incident happened simultaneously as Boko Haram used five French family members it kidnapped in border town of Nigeria and Cameroon as bargaining chips for the exchange of Boko Haram members captured by security agents in Nigeria.[4] These events unfolding now, Boko Haram's increasing terror attacks seemed to have been confirmed by the British Intelligence report that came out in 2009, two weeks prior to Boko Haram's outright declaration of 'jihad' to Islamize Nigeria.

WHO ARE BOKO HARAM?

Boko Haram was founded in 2002. It started its military-style operation in 2009 to create an Islamic state in Nigeria. Mohammed Yusuf, who was succeeded by Abubakar Shekau when Yusuf was killed in 2009 initially led the group. Boko Haram has referred to itself as the Nigerian Taliban. It seeks to overthrow the government and replace it with a regime based on Islamic law.[5]

Boko Haram, in Hausa language means, "Western education is sin." The group wants to carve out a separate Islamic state in Nigeria. However, it has targeted schools, as well as Christian churches and police and government offices, in its violent insurgence against the Nigerian state. Boko Haram has not hidden its intentions to transform Nigeria into a Sharia state with its own form of "Taliban" state domi nated by the extreme form of sharia laws. The group wants to achieve this goal even if it entails the use of deadly force to accomplish their mission.

Boko Haram has split into various factions. One of the prominent factions is the *Jama'atu Ahlis Sunna Lidda'awati wal-Jihad*, meaning in the same Hausa language "People Committed to the Propagation of the Prophet's Teachings and Jihad." Boko Haram and its splinter groups have three ideological positions, which make understanding each group's real objectives other than violence and taking innocent lives more difficult to comprehend. Boko Haram has commit violence under the common goal of imposing extreme sharia on Nigeria. While one group Boko Haram identifies with the Islamic brotherhood of Al-Qaeda and is inspired by Al-Qaeda transnational goals, the splinter group, Jama'atu Ahlis Sunna Lidda'awati wal-Jihad endorses the criminal activities that include kidnapping of foreigners and domestic political elites that opposed or challenged the fundamentalists or their ideologies.

Before Boko Haram, Nigeria witnessed its internal security threatened by Muslim extremists led by extremists including clerics. One of the most dreaded of the fundamentalists was the Mohammed Marwa group, also known as Maitatsine. The group leader, Marwa, was at the height of his notoriety during the 1970s and 1980s. He was sent into exile by the Nigerian authorities; he refused to believe Mohammed was the Prophet and instigated riots in the country, which resulted in the deaths of thousands of people. Some analysts view Boko Haram as an extension of the Maitatsine riots. [6]

BOKO HARAM TARGETS

Boko Haram targets include Nigerians – Christians and Muslims, Westerners and other foreigners in Nigeria. Three North Korean doctors serving at a hospital in Nigeria's northern Yobe state were killed early Sunday morning on February 10, 2013. The physicians were assisting at Potiskum General Hospital as part of a government agreement with the North Korean government towards implementing and improving health care in Northern Nigeria. The Sunday predawn slayings came on the heels of another deadly attack against medical workers.

On Friday, February 8, 2012, nine health workers who were administering polio vaccinations were killed in Kano, the biggest city in northern Nigeria. Boko Haram's splinter group , Islamic sect, *Jama'atu Ansarul Muslimina Fi Biladis Sudan* (also known as Ansaru) claimed responsibility for killing two Nigerian soldiers along the Lokoja-Okene road. The soldiers were on their way to Abuja to embark on a peacekeeping mission in Mali when they were ambushed and hacked to death. The same *Ansaru* also claimed responsibility for the kidnapped French national in Katsina when 11 foreign construction workers including Lebanese, British, Filipino and other nationals working at a Bauchi construction site were killed. Besides *Ansaru,* other breakaway factions robbed banks and financial institutions while others carried out killings for a price, no matter the individual or his standing in the society.[7]

The origin of Boko Haram and who is behind their financing remains unsubstantiated. President Jonathan has maintained that Boko Haram is proxies and supporters have infiltrated at all levels of his government. Speaking during an inter-denominational church service to mark the 2012 Armed Forces Remembrance Day, President Goodluck Jonathan remarked that some members of the sect were in the executive, legislative and judiciary arms of his government as well as the armed forces. "Some of them are in the executive arm of government; some of them are in the parliamentary/legislative arm of government while some of them are even in the judiciary.[8]

> "Some are also in the armed forces, the police and other security agencies. Some continue to dip their hands and eat with you and you won't even know the person who will point a gun at you or plant a bomb behind your house," the president alerted the nation. [9]

He disclosed that the situation has made it more difficult to combat the nation's security challenges head on. President Jonathan described the present security situation in the country as worse than the civil war experience, insisting, "This is a particular time when the country has major security challenges. There are explosions every day, people are dying and are being killed daily without any reason."[8]

Meanwhile, President Goodluck Jonathan has described as unfortunate, the alleged involvement and sponsorship of Boko Haram, by serving top politicians allegedly linked to the terrorist group. Dr. Goodluck was saying that all those behind the criminalization and politicization of what started as a religious organization would be made to face the wrath of the law. He spoke as fresh facts emerged that there could be more arrests of top political office holders in the weeks ahead, following what top security operatives described as conclusive evidence and intelligence gathering on the alleged link between the group and key sponsors.[9] No political office holder has been sentenced on account of supporting or financing Boko Haram jihadists. It was not until the kidnapping of the Chibok schoolgirls - with the international military and security experts' presence in Nigeria that some military generals and top politicians were interrogated as evidence of captured materials found at locations used by Boko Haram terrorists were allegedly linked to some political leaders in government.

However, the links of Northern politicians Boko Harm come not as a surprise as alleged connections began to emerge. An example of such links, apart from a senator Ali Ndume who was alleged to be connected to the terrorists was an incident on January 14, 2013. On this day, police arrested the suspected mastermind of the Boko Haram 2011 Christmas day bombing. The next day, the suspect escaped from detention. This incident occurred in broad daylight according to witnesses. The escape occurred as he was still wearing handcuffs. Authorities arrested, detained, suspended, and later dismissed a police commissioner for his alleged role in the escape of the suspect. The police commissioner eventually gained his freedom from custody, and there were no further updates on the case.[12] These unfolding events worried Nigerians who expressed concerns that the government could stop Boko Haram if it is determined to do so.

A Nigerian attorney, who wants to be identified only by his first name, Val said, "I think government knows the sponsors of Boko Haram but there is this belief rightly or wrongly that the initial sponsors are no longer in control and that they have lost control of the monster they created. Nevertheless, it takes political will to dig deeper – the political will to push security agents a bit harder. This government doesn't seem to have it in this regard."

While the sponsors of Boko Haram are sketchy, it is alleged that by association, the statements attributed to the Former Head of State and national leader of Congress for Progressive Change (CPC), Maj. Gen. Muhammadu Buhari that if he did not win the election, he would make Nigeria ungovernable for President Goodluck Jonathan. "Buhari had previously been credited with a statement that he would make the country ungovernable if the last presidential election did not favor him" - Senior Special Assistant to the President on Public Affairs, Dr. Doyin Okupe revealed in a press statement following interview Buhari had on the Hausa service of the British Broadcasting Corporation (BBC) on March 31, 2013 where he (Buhari) remarked that "The Federal Government should be blamed for the lingering security challenges in the country."[13] That statement, coupled with Buhari's silence on Boko Haram's military-style assaults, in particular Christian Churches bombing on Christmas and Easter eves by Jihadists made his critics claim Mohammadu Buhari knew more about the group and its activities than earlier speculated. Critics also alleged that Boko Haram has financial support from traditional and religious leaders in the North, the majority of whom have been the group persuading President Jonathan to grant amnesty to the Boko Haram members. General Buhari's suspicion of alleged sponsorship of the group focused not just on him but other Northern leaders.

Former Nigeria's Chief of Army Staff (COAS), Lt.-General Azubuike Ihejirika, disclosed Boko Haram's style of operation posed a serious challenge to security forces. Ihejirika disclosed the affiliation of the sect to Al Qaida in the Islamic Maghreb and Al-Shabaab has added an international dimension to the terrorists' membership, their organizational and military-styled operations. COAS said intelligence gathered about the group established that the Islamist sect declared its intent to Islamize the entire Northern states of Nigeria without regard to the constitution of the country. He noted that any country or community whose citizens had a high level of security awareness had higher chances of defeating terrorists.[14]

Whether it is in Afghanistan, Mali or Somali (Libya, Syria) and now Nigeria, the rise of insurgents such as Boko Haram adds a new perspective to violence trying to destabilize Nigeria and other African countries. As witnessed in Afghanistan, Somali and Mali, when these insurgents succeed in destabilizing the state, they are not just making it easy for their networks to have locations to migrate and occupy, the Jihadists would use the occupied spaces to prepare and launch an attack in new targets - other countries. Thus, they are only posing domestic risks, but also are endangerment to the peace and stability of the global village - particularly Jihadists attacking what they considered as Western values and influences they abhorred. The terrorists have never wavered in their interests to attack countries outside their control in particular, the United States and Europe.

As witnessed from Islamic extremists from countries in Afghanistan and the Middle East, the Jihadists never failed to include the United States and Europe as their targets in every opportunity they have used on the Internet or YouTube to relay their messages of hate. It also beats the imagination in Nigeria that few of the terrorists' attacks have been stopped due to intelligence gathering. Most of Boko Haram attacks in Nigeria were sporadic and often surprised authorities as they were to citizens, even when the insurgents issued warnings of their attacks ahead of time. Critics highlight that there were several warnings available that authorities should be able to dictate through intelligence where and if possible when terrorists could attack. It is no wonder that sharing information with US and other international intelligence is very important decision by President Jonathan's government. Experts agreed that the US, British, French, Canadian, and Israeli military and intelligence collaborators have the expertise and the experience to rescue the kidnapped Chibok schoolgirls, and tackle the problems posed by terrorists in West Africa.

Critics of Nigeria's government handling of Boko Haram's terrorism revealed that for the third time, on February 7, 2012, June 25, 2012 and March 14, 2013, the chief of the U.S. Africa Command, Army General Carter Ham warned of threats from Islamic extremists in Africa.[15] Gen. Ham told members of the House Armed Services Committee that if the threats posed by Boko Haram were not curtailed, the risks would increase, and if unchecked, could eventually pose a greater danger to the interests of the United States, and her allies. Gen Ham was being questioned by the committee on why it is important for a robust U.S. military involvement in Africa is necessary after more than a decade of war in Iraq and Afghanistan. Speaking about the danger posed to the U.S., not just Africa by terrorists in the region, Al-Qaeda in Mediterranean (AQIM)-linked terrorists are believed to have played a key role in the attack on September 11, 2012 I the U.S. diplomatic mission attack in Benghazi, Libya that killed four Americans, including U.S. Ambassador Chris Stevens." [16]

In Nigeria, Boko Haram continued to target state, religious, and international institutions as its targets. On March 2013, Boko Haram's splinter group *Jama a'tu Ansaru Muslimina Fi Baladis Sudan*, translated as "Vanguards for the protection of Muslims in Black Africa" claimed it killed 7 foreigners, hostages the Jihadist seized on February 7, 2013 from a construction company, Monitoring Services site in Northern Nigeria. Killed were a Briton, an Italian, a Greek and 4 Lebanese workers. The terror group showed screen shots of dead hostages they claimed were all Christians.[17]

While some Northern leaders claimed Boko Haram and its splinter groups were motivated by poverty, the translation of Boko Haram's name, meaning, "Western education is sin" and *Jama a'tu Ansaru Muslimina Fi Baladis Sudan*, translates as Vanguards for the protection of Muslims in Black Africa. The name ironically, has nothing to do with campaign against poverty inflicting Northern youth, the same youth it sends on suicide mission. Boko Haram's name concisely says a lot about what the group stands for. It is no wonder a cross-section of Nigerians were displeased with statements by some Western leaders such as former President Clinton and Human Rights Leader, Rev. Jesse Jackson suggested Boko Haram violence was caused primarily by the inequality in the distribution of wealth and youth unemployment in Northern Nigeria. [18]

Speaking to reporters in support of the decision by President Goodluck Jonathan to offer amnesty to members of Boko Haram, Jesse Jackson remarked the amnesty program (idea that was later discarded) if properly handled would tackle insecurity in Nigeria. However, he disclosed amnesty must involve economic restitution and rebuilding of mosques and churches destroyed by the terrorists.

"You can bargain and resolve the conflict in the North. That is why I believe so much in non-violence. Non-violence does not mean fear, but courage and thinking, and it means the ability to figure it out and fight it out."[19]

Nevertheless, considering that the North in Nigeria (Muslims) has produced majority of heads of states in Nigeria, and knowing the culture of marginalization, tribalism and favoritism in the allocation of resources in Nigeria based on the party in power or the tribe of the leader; it surprises some observers that these same leaders who have ruled Nigeria and they are from the North are the ones claiming that the uprising Islamic fundamentalists was as a result of 'poverty.' Critics asked who were in better position to have fought and reduced poverty than the leaders now complaining that poverty in the North was responsible for Boko Haram terrorism. "Anyway you look at the situation or the claims by these former leaders who claimed that insurgence is caused by poverty, it does not make sense," one anonymous critic remarked.

In hindsight, the marginalization of the South in Nigeria where the oil wealth of Nigeria is generated has been the root causes of political in fights between the South and North; with the South (mainly Christians) claiming that wealth from the South is the life support of Nigeria's economy. More so, there is the perception that the oil wealth is siphoned and used in developing the North to the disadvantage or complete neglect of the Southern States in Nigeria. This is at the same time that some critics also believed the revenue allocation to states whether North or South is not based on equity rather on population data that is an approximation and "deliberately" favored the North. The population data also used in the allocation of oil revenue is also said to be flawed as politicians from South claim that the real population of Northern States is based on projections and land mass and the data are unrealistic.

Since Northern Nigeria has produced more leaders from the North than South (the North have produced 13 head of states in Nigeria compared to four from the South since Nigeria's independence in 1960); it is based on this political advantage that critics expressed the States in the North should not have more disfranchised youth compared to States in the South. Critics claimed that it beats anybody's imagination, in particular any witness of Nigeria's history who has followed the politics of dichotomy and oil wealth distribution in Nigeria to think that the North that ruled Nigeria that long could claim victims when the reverse should be the case. Majority of Nigerians with access and ownership of auctioned oil wells in Nigeria are from the North. This is also worrisome when the North claims larger population than South, the statistics that the revenue allocation is allocated, and benefits Northern States more compared to South.

The argument is that same Northern elders and politicians who have been in control of national wealth complaining of youth marginalization of "their" Muslim population, then means they are passing judgment about their leadership record that never addressed the problems of the youth in the country (not just North – Muslims or South-Christians). A critic and a concerned Nigerian asked, "Who is therefore responsible for the poverty they are talking about that caused the youths to become terrorists?" "Northern (Muslim) youth's unemployment is not the reason why Boko Haram's terrorists are killing Christians, and Muslims that are against their jihadists' ideology and kidnapping school girls," he expressed.

The States in the North (Muslims) have produced dispropor

tionately more presidents in Nigeria than States in the South. About 13 head of states in Nigeria's 54 years after independence, only four – the late Aguiyi Ironsi, Ernest Oladeinde Shonekan, President Olusegun Obasanjo and President Goodluck Jonathan were Southerners and Christians.[20] General Yakubu Gowon was an only non-Muslim from northern Nigeria. He came from the middle belt, which some Northern political elites still don't consider as Muslim North rather middle belt because of its mixed Christians and Muslims population.

In essence, pundits disclosed that claim that the Northern youth are marginalized is not supported by any concrete evidence, as many Nigerians and observers of Nigeria's history also agreed that like the North, Southern youth have been marginalized by corrupt leaders that cared less about the people but about their pockets and cronies. In Nigeria where the South – Christians have accused the North of disenfranchising the South of oil wealth and using the foreign exchange earned from wealth of Nigeria coming from the South to develop Northern Nigeria (at the expense of Southern States), it means that the Northern youth have not benefitted from North leadership when they have and still occupy key positions at Federal government. It is at the federal government level that the allocation of huge revenue from oil to states every month for infrastructure development, salaries, jobs and other programs. These allocations are based on land mass and population – which the North has advantage over the Southern and Western States in Nigeria

A reflection on the internal politics and dynamics of oil revenue and distribution in Nigeria; an examination of the Nigeria landscape where upon all the wealth a country like Nigeria is endowed, about 60 percent of the population are in abject poverty - it indicates that poverty runs across the country whether North or South. That poverty seems more pronounced in the North is because of poor investment in education and entrepreneurship unlike the south. The evidence that such wealth is not benefiting youth in the North tells a lot about the characters of leaders that have ruled the people. Regrettably, some of the argument made by some of the Western leaders that the unemployment and marginalization of youth from the North is partly responsible for terrorism (re-echoing the opinions of Northern elders and politicians) are not convincing to a majority of Nigerians who wants to see an end to the shedding of precious blood of innocent people by terrorists.

Pundits also warned neither should anybody be persuaded by the argument that the reasons why Boko Haram has killed more than 12,000 people and it is still unrelenting in their assaults including the kidnapping of 300 Chibok school girls whose whereabouts is still unknown is because of poverty. In June, another set of 20 girls were kidnapped very close to Chibok Government Secondary school where the 300 school girls were previously kidnapped.[21] In August 15, 2014, Boko Haram kidnapped a group of young men in Doron Baga, a sandy fishing village in Borno state near the shores of Lake Chad.[22] This time, it took the Chadian Army to free about 75 of the boys while 25 of them are still held captive by their (Boko Haram) abductors.

Similarly, Boko Haram dispatched a female suicide bomber to an army barrack in Nigeria's northeastern city of Gombe on Sunday, June 8, 2014; the bomber's vest exploded killing a soldier, and a guard at the entrance of the military facility. The soldier was searching the vest of the suspect when explosives concealed under her hijab explod ed killing the guard. This happened as eyewitness reported over 110 death-counts in about a week from a string of earlier militant attacks in the area.[23] The reality from increasing frequency of these attacks [in spite of the presence of international military and intelligence experts to assist in the rescue of Chibok schoolgirls] is Boko Haram is unde-terred in escalating its campaign to impose strict Islamic laws on large-ly Muslim Northern Nigeria. While evidence showed that poverty ex-ists in Nigeria that causes violence or brings out violence in some peo-ple, the attacks on public property and lives by suicide bombers has nothing to do with poverty. Unfortunately, majority of their victims were poor and innocent Nigerians; the same could be said of young men and women terrorists sent out on suicide missions.

As the chief of the U.S. Africa Command, Gen. Carter Ham appealed, Nigeria needed international support to address the security problems spiraling out of control. General Ham made these pleas in more than three public events in the United States, before the congress and while speaking overseas including in Africa. His pleas was ful-filled when US. Britain, Canada, China, Israel (with Nigeria eventually accepting the assistance) sent technical and intelligence experts to as-sist Nigeria in the search and rescue of kidnapped Chibok school girls. It often takes a very long time for results to begin to emerge from this kind of rescue mission especially with the number of abducted victims.

The fears emerging after almost 4 months (still counting) of captivity, is that some of the kidnapped Chibok girls may have been assaulted, raped and some killed; others sent against the will on sui-cide mission. The fears began to emerge as the number of females, 12 -16 year old suicide bombers in month of July through early August 2014 reached an unprecedented level in the history of Boko Haram's deadly attacks on civilians and military personnel. The suspicion was that some of the abducted young girls who refused to change their religion or refused to be raped might have been killed in this manner. It was also gathered accomplice, who stood by, often accompanied these young suicide bombers and use remote control to detonate the improvised explosives strapped on these young girls sent on suicide mission. However, the pledge by President Jonathan to rescue all the girls alive and it was his decision that military force not be used to rescue the girls allows time for Nigeria and international tactical and intelligence team to weigh options that will not jeopardize the lives of the abducted school girls.

Waiting and weighing options are qualities of a good leader. However, there is no doubt Nigeria needs good leadership to build a virile economy, but pursuing these goals in an atmosphere of fear is impossible. President Jonathan has ambition to make Nigeria secured and reach its economic potentials; however, he with one of the brightest team of ministers Nigeria has ever produced may not succeed in an environment of terror and fear. Experts believe that for Nigeria to come out of this situation of insecurity it needs purposeful leadership with support of its people without politics, religion and social dichotomies that are prevailing in the country. Politics in particular has been the weakening link between the people and government causing setbacks and preventing Nigeria leaders from building the type of unity and cohesive team Nigeria needed to accomplish success, not just with its economy, but also eliminate the security risks posed by Boko Haram.

The global community also needs investors rather than donors to make Nigeria reach her full potential. Nigeria cannot afford to be a failed state. Poverty cannot be resolved by food and medical emergency assistances: U.S. or European aid of emergency food rather than help in sustainable development, which Africa needs to achieve lasting poverty reduction.[24]

Lloyd D. Black highlighted the need for U.S. to invest in Africa. Aside from the traditional U.S. humanitarian role, he pointed out that it is in the United States' interest to encourage and accelerate African development along constructive political, economic, and social lines, so African nations may become responsible, and progressive members of the Free World community. He remarked that the U.S. has strategic interests, both military and economic, in a number of African States. With China trade with African countries on the rise, the threat to US interests in Africa has become more threatened than ever before.

With copious human and natural resources - Nigeria like some other countries in Africa cannot be described as country in need of economic assistance. What Africa needs are trade opportunities, tariff-free market zones; quota for export of African products to Europe, Japan, and China. U.S. African agricultural cash crops and minerals are some of the areas of trade negotiations that present concentration on oil export from Nigeria and some oil – rich and gas exporting African nations is denying opportunities to explore these other business sectors. Describing Africa's situation as seen by an expert on Africa trade and business network, "Fish is already abundant; many are willing to catch as many fish as they can." However, government policies and international obstacles on closed doors, tariffs on trade and commerce do obstruct Africa traders (fishermen) from reaching the waters.

While African governments persuade their allies to open their doors to international trade, government must develop its educational system to support present and future development. In May 2011, the government released the findings of the 2010 Nigeria Education Data Survey, a follow-up report to the 2008 NDHS. According to the survey, attendance rates in primary schools ranged from 35 to 80 percent in Nigeria. The lowest attendance rates were in the Northeast and Northwest where rates for boys and girls hovered around 43-47 percent and 35-38 percent, respectively. Overall, 63 percent of boys and 58 percent of girls attended school. According to UNICEF, for every 10 girls in school, more than 22 boys attended school. For young persons between the ages of 17 and 25, about 25 percent had fewer than two years of education. Boko Haram was suspected to have caused the destruction of primary and secondary schools in Bornu and Yobe states. The attacks in Northeast and Central Nigeria have prohibited an unknown number of children from continuing their education[25]

Meanwhile, with the kidnapping of Chibok School girls and intensified Boko Haram terror attacks, Northern political and religious leaders demanding amnesty for Boko Haram Jihadists have drastically disappeared. President Goodluck Jonathan has rejected the idea even under pressure from Northern political and religious leaders wanting to persuade him along their recommendations to grant amnesty to Boko Haram terrorists. The leaders had claimed that the military response to quell the insurgence was not bringing peace to the region. They also claimed that similar militant group, the Movement for the Emancipation of the Niger Delta (MEND), based in the Southern part of the country that once terrorized Nigerians was granted amnesty in 2009 by the deceased Nigerian President Musa Yar'Adua, a northerner and a

Muslim. They argued that what is good for MEND should also be good for Boko Haram for peace and tranquility to reign. While the Northern leaders believed that amnesty should be extended to Boko Haram, majority of Nigerians has refused to see any similarity in goals MEND achieved and what Boko Haram is anticipated to achieve. However, it was not in doubt that thousands of MEND militants were granted amnesty by the Federal Government, in spite of the group's wreaked havoc in the oil-rich Niger Delta in southern Nigeria. The reason for irreconcilable differences between Boko Haram and MEND is that MEND was a political-militant group in Niger-Delta region where majority of Nigeria's oil and gas is drilled. MEND's mission was to expose and restrict the exploitation and oppression of the Niger Delta people. MEND also promotes using militant response to protect the Niger-Delta environment from pollution by oil drilling corporations. MEND perceived the Federal Government neglect of the devastation of the environment as collaboration between oil companies and the Nigeria federal government. They claimed that these corporations maintained high ethical and environment standards in their countries of origin in Europe and the United States, but government has allowed them to degrade the environment and hold nobody or company accountable for deaths and long-term environmental devastation that have everlasting implications on the environment and life of human and aquatic lives in the Niger-Delta area of Nigeria.

MEND also wanted a greater share of the oil revenue for the devastation caused by pollution on the people in the area. Majority of Niger-Delta citizens still live in abject poverty even as Nigeria oil revenue comes from their land with devastating pollution. The Federal government negotiated settlement that included special oil revenue allocation to the state, and negotiation with the oil corporations to protect the environment from future pollution.

CHAPTER 4

Boko Haram: The Real Financiers – The Financial Cash Flow, and Its Global Terror Networks

In 1998, there were simultaneous attacks on U.S. embassies in Dar es Salem, Tanzania and Nairobi, Kenya. Ten Kenyans and three Israelis, two of them children died from these attacks. As these incidents were taking place, two shoulder-Strela 2 (SA-7), surface-to-air missiles were launched by Al-Qaeda affiliated terrorists at another chartered Boeing 757 airliner owned by Israel-based Arkia Airlines. The plane was taking off from Moi International Airport, Kenya.

Before 9/11, terrorist attacks in Kenya and Tanzania took many African lives when U.S. embassies were targets. East Kenyan-born Fazul Abdullah Mohammed masterminded the attacks on the two embassies. The attacks brought attention to Bin Laden, who was declared the most wanted person in the world by the FBI. Al-Qaeda undoubtedly carried out the assaults in response to the United States involvement in the extradition and alleged torture of four Egyptian Islamic Jihad (EIJ) members arrested in Albania two months before the explosion in Kenya and Tanzania took place.

As witnessed the simultaneous patterns of terror attacks were the hallmark of Al-Qaeda. The 1998 bombings of the U.S. Embassies in Nairobi and Dar es Salaam, Tanzania killed 224 people, including 212 Africans, 12 Americans, and more than 5,000 were injured.[1] Africans were majority of the victims in these attacks. As acknowledged by President Obama when he addressed youth on June 2013 speech at Soweto in Johannesburg, South Africa, victims of terrorist attacks are more often the local people, not the West or foreigners as terrorists often express in their rhetoric. With all these terror attacks in Africa including Al-Shabaab in Somalia, Al_Qaeda in the Mediterranean (AQIM) operating across Tunisia, Algeria, Mali and Libya, and now Boko Haram in Nigeria, not much attention in the war against terror has been focused on the continent, rather on Afghanistan, Iraq and Pakistan. The fight against terror from these spaces has dominated the attention and commended huge military expenditures to confront terrorists in these countries. Though there is a strong network of Al-Qaeda in Somalia and across countries in West African region, the superior military power and other logistic assets on the command of Boko Haram according to experts were made possible because of the neglect or under-rating of the Jihadists by Nigeria government and world leaders. Therefore, when on June 2, 2013, the United States posted a $23 million reward for information that would lead to the arrest of five leaders of terrorists in West Africa; the U.S. State Department Rewards for Justice Program identified the fugitives as the masterminds of terror in the region. It was well-received news and a turning point on the fight against terrorists. The decision also marked for the first time bounties were posted for wanted terrorists in West Africa, it gave hope that the US is eventually paying attention to the atrocities committed by Boko Haram and its other networks in the region. While some politicians in the United States and pundits believed that the bounties were overdue, others welcome the development as a step forward to putting pressure on the terrorists in the African region. The decision sent a strong message to the Boko Haram and its splinter groups that the world is watching.

The biggest amount in terms of reward, about $7 million was offered for information leading to Boko Haram's leader, Abubukar Shekau arrest, along with another $5 million each for Al-Qaeda veteran Moktar Belmokhar, elderly French hostage-taker in Nigeria. The declaration by the State Department of these men as "Most Wanted Fugitives" showed not just concerns of how dangerous the one-eye Islamist behind the Algerian gas plant attack in January was but others as well. About 37 foreigners including three Americans were killed during attack on the Algerian oil refinery, which the Jihadists wanted to take over. AQIM leader, Yahya Abou Al-Hamam was also involved in the murder of others including tourists. He was also a key player in the global networks of Boko Haram terrorists that include technical, military and financial network collaborations. These connections of terrorist groups are serious concerns to Nigeria government and the United States State Department.

A week before the United States placed the bounties on the suspected terrorists; Boko Haram called on the Islamists in Afghanistan, Pakistan, and Iraq to join the bloody fight to create an Islamic state in Nigeria.[2] The same outreach call was made by Boko Haram leader Abubakar Shekau to Al-Qaeda in the Islamic Maghreb, Afghanistan, and Pakistan when in May 2013, the Federal Government sent troops to combat the terror. The terror group also made a similar call for support to Al-Qaeda when their members (terrorists) were pounded by Nigeria's Joint Military Task Force with both air and land raids. This was in the same month of May 2013.

On July 12, 2014, Boko Haram also sent a solidarity message to Islamic State of Iraq and Syria (ISIS) for the Islamic militant group setting up a self-proclaimed Islamic Caliphate in the region. "My brethren... may Allah protect you," Shekau said in the video given to AFP, listing ISIS chief, Abu Bakr al-Baghdadi, Al-Qaeda head Ayman al-Zawahiri and Taliban leader Mullah Omar."[3] Shekau claimed responsibility for a June 25, 2014 bombing in the capital city of Abuja and another attack hour later in Lagos, which the authorities in Lagos tried to cover up. ISIS is known for its brutal violence directed at Shia Muslims and Christians. The Islamic organization is also known for its extreme Wahhabist interpretation of Islam.

These liaisons notwithstanding, re-examination of Boko Haram's ideology posted on its website revealed a domestic terror group based in Northern villages in Bornu State, Nigeria. It was founded on the same philosophy of using terror to achieve its goal of Islamizing Nigeria, and at the same time destabilize the country while using Nigeria as a base to reach its targets in the West, particularly the United Kingdom and the United States.

In its mission statement, Boko Haram declared itself as a congregation of people committed to the propagations of the Prophet's teachings and jihad in the Nigeria Sharia conflict. It has as its ideology – Islamic extremism, Islamic fundamentalism or *Tafir*; its area of operations is Northern Nigeria, Northern Cameroon, Niger and Chad; its allies is Al-Qaeda in the Islamic Maghreb; its opponents – Nigeria State. Battle – included the Nigeria Sharia conflict and 2009 Nigeria sectarian violence.

These words were in verbatim what Boko Haram revealed it represented and ideologies it stood for, and more. Boko Haram terrorists have kidnapped and slaughtered Nigerians and Westerners. These are part of the extremist Islamists mission. The fact that its name translates to "Western Education is sin" but was not included in its motto on display on its website and on the YouTube shows a terror group whose agenda has over time expanded. Boko Haram is not in any way relenting in its blood bath and killing of innocent citizens by using sophisticated commandos, military–style weapons and suicide bombings to achieve its goals.

Boko Haram's goal of destabilizing the government and creating an Islamic State in Nigeria drives its links to Al-Qaeda and Al-Shabaab and other international networks and vice versa. Its connection to these networks has also been the same motivation for its global outreach for funding, even though there were not enough evidence to link Boko Haram to Al-Qaeda finances in Iraq, Afghanistan and Syria. In essence, several links to these international terror organizations have expanded the financial outreach by the Jihadists who originally started raising money through individual members' contributions.

The membership contributions started in 1995, when the terror group operated under the name Shabaab - a Muslim youth organization (adaptation of Shabaab of Somalia's name). At the period, Mallam Lawal was its leader. When Lawal left the youth organization to further his education, the group, under its new leader, Mohammed Yusuf, turned into a political organization. Under Yusuf, the group also received donations from notable Muslims in the North. One particular prominent donor donated a bus and loud speakers to the organization. Mohammed Yusuf's father-in-law, Baba Fugu, donated a farm at Auno village in Konduga, a Local Government Area of Borno State. The farm was later converted to the group's first training camp.[4]

Among Boko Haram's major sponsors was a "businessman" from Bauchi State in Nigeria who already has a link with Al-Qaeda in Somalia. He was alleged to have received training from Abu Umar Al-Wadud, the leader of Al-Qaeda in Somalia. It was gathered the businessman escaped in 2009 following the attack by security agencies in Nigeria to flush out Boko Haram leaders and dislodge the group. Thus, he was forced to relocate to Somalia.

When Nigeria was returning to democratic rule in 1999, and the political campaign was on a new starting point, some local politicians were supporting extreme Islamic manifestos and policies in the North states of Nigeria. Some gubernatorial candidates were openly contesting on the manifestoes that they will introduce sharia and Islamize Northern Nigeria if elected into office. At the time, there were no Jihadists, but political thugs and organizations that could turn into fundamentalists groups were evolving and seeking sponsors.

In fact, the campaign to introduce sharia across Northern States came to fruition in October 22, 1999 when Sanni Ahmed Yerima, then an elected Governor of Zamfara State made the initial announcement to his constituents his introduction of Sharia in the state. He followed his promise to the citizens and presented a Sharia bill that passed into law in Zamfara in January 2000. Governor Yerima's determination to further introduce Islamic laws and press for extreme form of sharia laws were not in doubt. It was his political rally point for his voters that saw him in office as a governor in 1999. Yerima also needed foot soldiers to standby against opponents, and on a short notice provide a matching [Jihadists] army to execute his jihadists' agenda in the state.

Between 1999 and 2000, Ahmed Yerima led 14 other Northern states in Northern Nigeria to adopt Sharia laws in their states. The success of his moves gave new momentum for fundamentalists that have now role models in these state executives for their own agenda and awakened interests that introducing extreme forms of sharia is a possible task in the 14 states and across Nigeria.

Meanwhile, some politicians found common grounds to associate with the Jihadists, which in 2002 adopted the name Boko Haram. Boko Haram under the leadership of Mohammed Yusuf opened the group to political influence and popularity in 2002 as these political campaigns were going on, hoping to win elections, but with the bigger goal of introducing a sharia state in Bornu State. As revealed by Yusuf when the group was launched in Maiduguri, Boko Haram's goal was always to establish a sharia state in Bornu State. With financial support from Ali Modu Sheriff, who later became the Governor of Bornu State, the groups expanded its powers. A testimony that Boko Haram's emergence and funding have political undertones came with the statement by Boko Haram's member arrested on November 3, 2011 by the operatives of State Security Service. In a op editorial article by the Associate editor of the *Nation,* Taiwo Ogundipe, a Boko Haram member identified as Ali Sanda Umar Konduga alias Usman al-Zawahiri (named after the leader of Al-Qaeda after the death of Osama Bin Laden) unraveled the riddle about the funding of the Boko Haram.

According to Konduga's testimony (through an interpreter, Mohammed Yusuf), Boko Haram's late leader, Yusuf, who died while in police custody in 2009, trained him. He also revealed that Boko Haram had origins in a militia group known as ECOMOG. The name is an adaptation of the military arm of the Economic Community of West African States (ECOMOG) known for its military interventions to bring peace in the West African region. Boko Haram's ECOMOG was a political youth militant group formed in 2003. The ECOMOG provided Boko Haram more members and military training. The Presidential Committee on Security Challenges in the North-East Nigeria, chaired by Ambassador Usman Galtimari, has disclosed that ECOMOG created the fertile ground for the speedy growth and the spread of Boko Haram.[5]

Boko Haram member identified as Ali Sanda Umar Konduga alleged that former Governor Sheriff was the financier of the group at a point. He disclosed that an ex-Governor Sheriff even appointed their leader, Fugi Foi, as a commissioner in the state. "When Foi was sacked and then killed, the sect believed that his death was political and swore to avenge it." He disclosed that it was then that the late Saidu Pindar, Nigeria Former Ambassador to Sao Tome and Principle stepped in as a major financier of the sect and promised them N10 million. Konduga, alias Al-Zawari, revealed that Pintar was on his way to deliver N5 million to Boko Haram when he had a motor accident and died.[6]

Pintar died on August 31, 2011 along Kaduna –Zaria road. Before his death, he sought election under People Democratic Party (PDP) as a running mate to the gubernatorial candidate, Mohamadu Goni. Konduga revealed that it was Pintar that nicknamed him Al-Zawahiri to conceal his (Konduga) identity for security reasons.[7] Konduga also said that a serving Senator in the Federal Republic of Nigeria, Mohammed Ali Ndume later took over the sponsorship of the sect after Pintar's death.[8] Ndume was a two-term member of the House of Representatives on the platform of All Nigeria People's Party

(ANPP). He also served as a Minority Leader of his party in the House of Representative before he joined the People' Democratic Party (PDP) in 2011 in order to contest for the Senate in 2011, which he won. Ndume was arrested by State Security Service in Nigeria and was detained and later freed. Senator Ndume has denied any of these connections.

Sources revealed that Boko Haram's financing could also be traced to Kano and Bauchi states. According to an unnamed interviewee, a member of the Boko Haram held in detention by the Nigeria State Security Services (SSS) disclosed that the former Governor of Kano State, Ibrahim Shekarau had promised in 2004 to make an initial monthly payment of $5 million to the group. The sources alleged that he later raised the monthly payment to N10 million. He disclosed that apart from these monthly payments, the government of Shekarua provided institutional infrastructure support through the *Hisbah* (Islamic Police) project, which received an annual budgetary allocation of N1.01 billion. All these promises, including the funding of the "Islam Police," were stopped when a new Governor of the State, Rabiu Kwankwaso took over power in Kano State.[9]

The detainee also revealed that in Bauchi state similar agreement was reached between Boko Haram and the incumbent Governor Isa Yuguda in 2008 for a monthly payment of N10 million. The agreement, the source disclosed, included the provision of training grounds on the mountains scattered in Bauchi State, in addition to guaranteed protection against arrest by the Federal Government. The detainee said that the Bauchi State Governor stopped the monthly funding in mid-2011, but the group was not aggrieved because of the access the state offered the members to use the mountain tops located in the state for training. However, he remarked that since the group was not happy with the development involving the termination of their monthly payments and *Hisbah,* Islamic Police project, the group still decided to wage massive assaults on Kano Metropolis and Bauchi city leading to the deaths of hundreds of people.

While the two state governments mentioned denied their involvement, Boko Haram's spokesperson remarked, "Northern Governors are overwhelmed about the strength of the group and are aware of the capabilities of Boko Haram operatives in the prospective states." Some of the state government officials the interviewee disclosed "visited their camps to watch them in training exercises. The training is harder than that of the Nigerian military."[10]

All Nigeria Peoples Party (NPP) former Deputy Chairman, and a retired General in the Nigeria Armed Forces, Brigadier Genial Jeremiah Useni (rtd.), while on a visit to Borno State, witnessed many young people selling petroleum products in the open streets, and he asked the Governor, why the young people were allowed to engage in illegal trading in petroleum products? The Governor's response was "...leave them, they are useful to us (during general elections as thugs), we use them to turn everywhere meaning to stir trouble."[11]

Meanwhile, the Joint Military Task Force detained the chairman of the All Nigeria Peoples Party (ANPP in Bornu State), Mala Othman over the suspicion that he has links with the *Jamaá Ahl a-sunnah lida'wa wa al-jihad*, better known by its Hausa name as Boko Haram. Othman's arrest followed the July 2013 attack of 30 students of Federal Government College.[12] Potiskum town, Yobe state was invaded in the early morning hours with many male students slaughtered by gunmen suspected to be Boko Haram. Othman's house was also set ablaze by the youth volunteer group christened "Civilian JTF" but also identified as "Vigilante Youth Against Boko Haram."

Since Boko Haram is considered a major political threat to Nigeria, Africa Command (AFRICOM) Commander, General Carter F. Ham confirmed in September 2011 that the terror group with other African and global terror groups are targeting Westerners and specifically, the U.S. He disclosed the synchronization of efforts entailed raising funds across international boundaries to achieve their goals. While Boko Haram's funding is local, it seemingly enjoyed the same international support from the United Kingdom and Saudi Arabia. Replacing the Afghanistan' situation in Nigeria entailed funding from across the world including some Islamic organizations such as Al Muntada Trust Fund with headquarters in the United Kingdom and the Islamic World Society with headquarters in Saudi Arabia. [13]

Boko Haram is linked to the global and trans-national criminal activities that include kidnapping for ransom, drug trafficking, weapons trafficking and armed robbery.[13] Former chief of Nigeria Army Staff (COAS), Lt General Azubuike Ihejirika told reporters in an interview that the Army did recognize the involvement of foreigners in the operation of Boko Haram. He said that the weapons and other sophisticated military ammunitions captured from the group did establish foreign backers to the group. He said these are strong evidence of foreign involvement in the acts of terrorism taking place in Nigeria. "The types of weapons we have captured, the type of communication equipment and the expertise Boko Haram has displayed in the preparation of improvised explosives devices…these are pointers to the fact that there is international involvement in the terrorism going on in Nigeria."[14]

When then Senator Ali Modu Sheriff built a mosque and established an Islamic school, he opened the doors to the school to poor families from across Nigeria and neighboring Niger and Chad – two countries with open borders to Nigeria. The goal of sending these children to the Islamic Center was according to sources, to train these teenagers in extreme form of Islamic (sharia) principles. However, the objective quickly shifted to using the center for training of future Jihadists to fight several causes they may be sent including fighting politicians and the state of Nigeria. Such schools have been known to exist in Afghanistan and Iraq, and their financial outreach and assistance from Islamic organizations and institutions around the world are not limited to Europe and Saudi Arabia.

Boko Haram has never wavered in executing its national and international agenda, some members of the terrorist group apprehended by federal security agents in Nigeria revealed that the group depended on donations by members, fundamentalists' politicians in the Northern States for their operation. Boko Haram's link with Al-Qaeda in the Islamic Maghreb (AQIM) and Al-Qaeda in the Middle East has added more to the channels of funding for the group with far outreach to other Islamic organizations in United Kingdom and Saudi Arabia. [15]

While Boko Haram continued to wreak havoc - destruction that costs both human lives and loss of property in billions of dollars, the attempt by the federal government to dislodge, and probably dislodge the terror network seemed to be gradually yielding results. The Joint Task Force that included all the arms of Nigeria military, police, air force and State Secret Service have put the terror group on the run. While the group has dispersed, it most times rallies members together in small numbers and continues to engage in sporadic killings using Motorcycles and open confrontation with the Joint Military Task Force comprising the State Secret Service (SSS), the military and police. These attacks seemed endless in spite of the Federal Government's declared state of emergency Yobe, Nassarawa, Borno and other curfews that limited movements in neighboring states at specific hours of the day.

However, upon the intensified effort by authorities in Nigeria to dislodge Boko Haram (this was before the invitation of international technical and security experts to rescue the kidnapped Chibok schoolgirls), locating and stopping the group's financial links remain a daunting task? The intentions by Federal Government of Nigeria to introduce paperless money transactions in key states in Nigeria are part of the efforts to control the flow of cash to the terror groups. However, as pundits have disclosed, most of the financial transactions by terror groups are by cash, either through the black market or underground economic transactions. Because of a lack of efforts and because of bureaucratic bottlenecks to overcome in Nigeria, getting governments across Nigeria borders and banking institutions to sign into the agreement to retrain or stop money laundry across these borders remains very difficult task to accomplish. Meanwhile, capital flight including money going to Boko Haram and other terrorist organizations in Africa and Middle East continue to flow uninterrupted.

A threat to blacklist Nigeria was made by the international anti-monetary laundering watchdogs over Nigeria's inability to track the sources of funds, including money transactions by dreaded Islamic group, Boko Haram. The Financial Action Task Force (FAFT), an organization renowned for setting the global standards for measures to combat money laundering, terrorism and proliferation financing, disclosed that Nigeria was not cooperating despite early warnings for the country to comply with the rules. In its report in May 2012, FAFT listed Nigeria among the countries that have not made any significant progress in addressing the huge problems identified by Anti-Money Laundering and Combating Terrorism Financing (AML/CTF) regimes.[16]

On May 2014, Human Rights group - Socio-Economic Rights and Accountability Project (SERAP) urged the United Nations Security Council to move swiftly and impose targeted sanctions against Boko Haram attacks against children and other civilians. According to SERAP, "Sanctions send a powerful signal to the perpetrators and contribute to greater compliance with the Council's agenda on children in armed conflict," [17] SERAP also requested the Security Council to consider a broad range of options for increasing pressure on Boko Haram and their backers. It is anticipated the sanctions will contribute and reduce the continuous attacks and abuse of children by the extremist group, and assist Nigeria in the fight to combat terrorism. SERAP said that sanctions would increase international action to reduce the impunity with which Boko Haram operates. International terrorism experts agreed that the decision could mark a turning point to secure the safe return of the missing schoolgirls and secure Nigeria and the region from being run over by Jihadists.

CHAPTER 5

Boko Haram - Exploiting the Art of Propaganda & Media Publicity

---

Boko Haram, Al-Qaeda in the Middle East and the Al-Shabaab in Somalia, enjoy media publicity. They use the media also to recruit new members. With the international media focusing attention on the group, Boko Haram utilizes the opportunity to the full and even goes the extra length to feed the media with You-tube videos as part of its propaganda effort. Unfortunately, Boko Haram has often received more attention than individuals have and their family members who were killed or maimed by suicide bombers dispatched by the terror group. The free media publicity also gives the Jihadists opportunities to recruit followers.

There is no doubt a victim from Jihadists' assaults, and their families deserved more attention in the media than the terrorists receive. As evidence showed including the frequency of their attacks on the news cycle, the terrorists were more often in the news for the wrong reasons. Not only are these jihadists in the headline news, they also continue their bombing and blood-bath even at a time there was pressure on the Federal Government of Nigeria to set up an amnesty committee at the cabinet level of government to consider whether to negotiate an amnesty with the group. Though President Jonathan declined to negotiate with the insurgents, there was no clear direction of the amnesty – meaning under what conditions and for what purposes amnesty should be that include in the negotiations to avoid more bloodshed. Northern elders (religious and political), along with some Southern politicians have mounted pressure on President Jonathan to look into the option of granting members of Boko Haram amnesty. Supporters of the amnesty initiative believed it would reduce deaths and security threats that the group posed to the national security of Nigeria.

However, as the negotiations for the amnesty was then on its way to manifesting (even as pro-amnesty were sure the president would change his mind and eventually grant the amnesty), Boko Haram continued their attacks on civilians, police, military and government agencies and institutions. Boko Haram also issued threats to media organization that do not give them publicity or its leader perceived as biased or subjective. In other words, the terror group considered any media that does not report the activities of the terror group "objectively" as its "enemy" despite the disastrous bloodbath and deaths on the streets, across Northeast and Central Nigeria that media highlighted.

Boko Haram was conveying the message that in spite of the bloodbath unleashed on Nigerians, and the security threat the group poses to the stability of Nigeria, its leaders are not satisfied that the media was paying more attention to deaths and not what causes those carrying arms to attack innocent citizens. In the mindset of terrorists, the group's leader Abubakar Shekua has warned the media of disastrous consequences any attempt by reporters to report 'subjectively' about the activities of the terrorists. They also warned the media about feeding the federal government information about Boko Haram.

Shekau went further to cite the experience of *This Day* newspaper in 2002 when pre-Miss World fundamentalists rioted and razed the newspaper Miss Isioma Daniel was working as a reporter and columnist for the paper. She had in a satirical article queried why the Miss World pageant rioters were destroying lives (200 Nigerians were killed) just because they were against hosting a beauty pageant. She postulated that that they should stop the rioting suggesting that after all, Prophet Mohammed would have liked the show to go on, and may have even taken one of the contestants as a bride. The article was perceived as blasphemous.

Boko Haram leader Abubakar Shekau warned news organizations not reporting events about his Jihadist organization "accurately" they will face the same consequences as *ThisDay* (the newspaper Ms. Daniel who wrote the article on Mohammed worked in 2002). Shekau's threat was that any newspaper reporting "subjectively" about Boko Haram and its activities will be razed down and the journalists killed. Daniel, a young columnist, fled to Norway when fundamentalists declared Fatwa on her head following her satirical article on *This Day* newspaper that queried the rioting against the 2002 Miss World pageant in Nigeria.

The fundamentalists have opposed the pageant as Western hedonism and culture that disrespects women by exposing publicly women nudity, which the jihadists claimed is against sharia law. The rioters killed 200 Nigerians and forced the organizers of the Miss World pageant to cancel the event. It was later held in Alexandria Hall in the heart of London instead of Abuja. The preliminary sessions of the pageant had concluded in Abuja and other locations including Calabar, in Cross Rivers State in the southern part of the country. The finals were taking place when the rioting erupted in Kaduna and later spread to Abuja.

Boko Haram contradictory philosophy and its action are part of a ploy by the group to gain media attention. For example, in January 2012, Abubakar Shekau claimed that the group was carrying out attacks on Christians in retaliation for the killing of Muslims by Christians in central Nigeria, including Kaduna and Plateau states during sectarian violence. Boko Haram leader 'Imam Abubakar Shekau' sent a message to the president through YouTube 'Message to President Jonathan.'[1] Similarly, on December 24, 2010 following attacks on Christmas-eve mass in the cities of Jos and Maiduguri, Boko Haram released a statement claiming the attacks were to avenge "atrocities committed against Muslims.[2]

Once, Boko Haram "disparaged" and "disliked" Western technology, but now found it useful in their violent attacks on civilian targets. In practice, cellular phones, automobiles, video cameras, YouTube and the Internet have been effective in their propaganda to win members and propagate their ideologies, which, unfortunately, the media is indirectly assisting the group by the frequency of publicity they receive. Boko Haram's use of modern technology and the mediated media to get their messages across has been unfortunately successful in getting their messages of blood assaults and terror on the population.

Since 2009 when Boko Haram, the terrorists commenced their suicide bombing and kidnapping, it has not conceded in using the media as a propaganda tool to inform authorities before or after they carried out attacks. The pattern of using the media before and after attacks took place was witnessed with Boko Harm's Easter Sunday attack of a Catholic Church in the city of Kaduna. More than 36 people were killed by a suicide bomber riding in bomb-loaded vehicle.[3] Boko Haram has also unleashed a 42-month multi-pronged attack on military, police and security facilities, and churches that claimed more than 3000 lives. [4]

Boko Haram Jihadists have also claimed responsibility using the media to publicize their assaults including suicide bombings. The group has also killed and kidnapped some Westerners as hostages and used the media to publicize their kidnapping and even their release whether by negotiation or payment of ransom. With the French and Malian troops engagement in Northern Sudan (which successfully led to the flushing of the Jihadists out of Mali and the flight of their descendants into the desert while others infiltrated the general public and neighboring states), the danger the Jihadists pose to Nigeria and other African countries' internal security cannot be underestimated.

Boko Haram fighters are dreaded because they have more sophisticated military weapons in their armory than soldiers going after the terrorists. Some of them were traceable to the fall of Libya and the looting of ammunition depots by the public; others were military ammunitions including armored vehicles, shoulder rocket launchers and surface-to-air missiles captured either during attacks on the military and police posts or during their frequent invasions and attacks on military barracks and installations. The lack of attention to protect the arms getting into the wrong hands such as Al-Qaida and other radical groups was what pundits claimed the media missed during the Libyan revolution that ousted Muommer Gadhafi. The media was occupied with the overthrow of Gadhafi and not with the security of Libya, the region, and Africa. The media, the pundits highlight, is showing the same pattern of reporting by not addressing where the insurgents – the jihadists had fled with their weapons. The media is once again focusing attention on French presence in Mali, its historical implication based on post-colonial experiences of Mali and the France's relationships with the government and people of Mali; and whether the French are staying or leaving Mali soon.

These are important historical commentaries; however, pundits explained that when these issues are the focus, insurgents disappear from the news radar. Similarly, when the media fails to track the movement of insurgents either overwhelmed by government forces and they decided to disappear or fade into the public, the society is in more endangered than when the terrorists are captured or killed. The fear that these terrorists will emerge somewhere in the country or neighboring state explains why there is uncertainty which country will be the next target of the Jihadists. It is no wonder; pundits believe that these terrorists have mastered the art of disappearing and resurfacing in countries across Africa and Middle East. This is a major security threat in West Africa and African region has exacerbated because nobody is tracking these Jihadists' movement with their arms and money to the next space they will invade and occupy.

The situation explains why there has been call for a new international media order in reporting Africa in the 21st century. The old-style of reporting of Africa by the media to appeal to a local audience in their homeland in an era of Information Communication Technology (ICT), and with mediated media, needs a paradigm shift in ways and style international media report Africa.

BOKO HARAM AND THE CONSPIRACY THEORISTS

Nigeria is an oxymoron. It is a country endowed with abundant human and material resources, yet it seems she is incapable using those abundant human and material resources to help better the lives of majority of her own people. With the Boko Haram's terror attacks, there is a rise and the spread of conspiracy theories among people across its ethnic lines that Boko Haram is a creation of the West to achieve the agenda of Nigeria failed State, other conspiracy, even accuse the Nigeria President Jonathan of being "commander in chief" of Boko Haram. The accusation of the president has alleged connection to Boko Haram is mostly from opposition, who the president publicly said some of their members knew about the people behind Boko Haram including some members of his inner circles (his executive).

With distractions by these conspiracy theories and the strong belief by some that they are true, they add to the problems that impede Nigeria's development. Apart from Boko Harm's conspiracy theories, others have floated for decades even before Boko Haram emerged on the scene. People, mainly Southerners allege that Northern leaders (Muslims) were "milking" Nigeria oil to develop the North –to the disadvantage or neglect of the South. These conspiracy theorists believed that the North is involved in this tactics so that they could finally declare their own Islamic country governed by sharia laws. That long-planned mission, the conspiracy theorists believe is being fulfilled by Boko Haram fighting for the cause – "the Islamization of Nigeria" through any means including by violence.   The theorists also believe that when Sanni Ahmed Yerima, then an elected Governor of Zamfara

State presented a Sharia Bill to the House of Assembly and it was passed into law in Zamfara in January 2000, it was a successful motivation to Jihadists that have long awaited opportunities. When in between 1999 and 2000, Ahmed Yerima led 14 other Northern states in Northern Nigeria to adopt Sharia laws in their states, Yerima and the States that adopted sharia needed foot soldiers – those "soldiers" according to conspiracy theorists led to formation of new fundamentalist groups and motivation for existing ones. One of them has metamorphosed and grew out of control in the name of Boko Haram.

There are also conspiracy theory that believed the prediction by Western pundits that Nigeria will be a failed state in 2015 adds more suspicion to what causes tensions in Nigeria, including Boko Haram fighters that pose serious threat to internal security of Nigeria. Boko Haram has gone the length in ensuring that Nigeria is a failed state. According to several statements attributed to Boko Haram members and obtained from eyewitnesses including those by Human Rights Watch in 2012, the terror group no doubt is striking at Christians for many reasons. Boko Haram claims that they attack "Christians to avenging the atrocities committed against Muslims," undermine "disbelievers and their allies and all those who support them," [5] and "liberate ourselves and our religion from the hands of infidels and the Nigerian government" as part of a "full scale war between the Muslims and the Christians."[6]

Boko Haram violence against Christians has included the torching and blowing up of churches, and carrying out abductions, forced conversions, and attacks in markets and during religious services using guns, improvised explosive devices, or suicide bombers. During the July 2009 assaults, for example, witnesses in Maiduguri said that Boko Haram fighters torched churches, killing men hiding inside the holy place. They also abducted Christians and took them to Yusuf's compound. Boko Haram members also killed Christian men after they refused to convert to Islam.[7]

Boko Haram's attacks on Christians has resulted in deaths, and forced conversion of Christians to Islam. They have also sparked sectarian clashes in already volatile states. On three successive Sundays in June 2012, for example, suicide bombers detonated explosives at church services in Bauchi, Bauchi State; Jos, Plateau State; and Zaria and Kaduna, These states in Nigeria are also locations of past episodes of inter-communal violence.[8] The attacks on two churches in Zaria and a church in Kaduna killed at least 21 people, and set off several days of reprisal and counter-reprisal killings. The clash between Christians and Muslims resulted in 80 more deaths.[9] Similarly, the Christmas Eve 2010-bomb blasts in Christian communities in Jos sparked a month of sectarian bloodletting that claimed around 200 Muslim and Christian lives.[10]

Amidst staggering corruption and mismanagement of resources by political leaders, a cross section of Nigerians believe that politicians "fabricate" some of these conspiracy theories to distract the masses while they loot the system. For Boko Haram, there is the conspiracy of "the West to Rule the World by destroying Islam. First, there is no doubt conspiracy theories are not particular to Nigeria. There are individuals worldwide who believe in one conspiracy or the other. Either they believe, for example, that 6 out of the 19 hijackers that flew jets into the World Trade Center in the U.S. are alive or they believe that it was not terrorists, but "others" who did it. Others believe that the 911 attack was the U.S. government's conspiracy to go to war and occupy

Iraq and maintain their presence in Middle East or/and for the sake of oil.

Similarly, some believed that the idea of Apollo Moon landing was a real or a hoax. However, for humans, as long as they exist, there are bound to be ordinary men and women, who are fairly or unfairly motivated to believe what they want to. However, it becomes troubling when such unfounded and unsubstantiated beliefs are made real, disseminated to persuade people against the West, and use such baseless propaganda to recruit future terrorists in Nigeria or elsewhere.

However, political elites and clerics that frame these conspiracy theories in their efforts to persuade and win converts to their side should not be taken for granted. For instance, in Nigeria where Boko Haram has gained ground, the teaching of clerics that see others not holding their religious views as "infidels" and must be 'converted' or 'destroyed' seem to be working especially since there are no institutions established either by the state or Christian religious organizations and institutions to counter these erroneous "religious ideologies."

In Northern Nigeria, some religious organizations use videos that are ant-West to teach their pupils. Some of these religious clerics and politicians sometimes go the length of distributing the anti-West videos to Christians for reason that may include either seeking new converts or as their own personal or groups campaign to show the West that Nigerians in the South or West welcoming Western values and education are "traitors." In all circumstance, the goal of clerics spreading these propaganda materials and conspiracy theories have their goal of reaching out to the youth whose mind are still not developed, but have the trust reposed by the parents of the youth that the clerics are teaching their children to be upright Muslims. As evidence from suspected and convicted terrorist arrested in either Britain or the United States have shown, these were youth indoctrinated by their mullahs to commit crimes that the young people may not be willing to do or carry out on their own.

The steps taken by fundamentalists to brainwash young people, the process has been gradual and evidence showed that they have been successful in radicalizing good number of youth in Northern Nigeria. In some circumstances, the youth were self-radicalized by their peers whose goal is to destroy infidels (innocent lives) because of lessons they were taught in their so-called religious school, Another propaganda mechanism employed by the extremists to indoctrinate the youth is the frame that Islam is under constant attack by "Powers" that want to rule the world by destroying religious values Muslims hold very strongly. The youth are encouraged to resists and challenge the "Powers" that want their religion extinct at all costs and the defense will improve the chances of Islam's survival. In essence, the fight to resist the influence of these "Powers" and the survival for their religion and culture means defending their religion even at the expense of lives of the Jihadists.

Regrettably, there is no particular place that this mentality of using conspiracy theory as a recruitment tool more than in "religious" schools" in Nigeria where countries in the Middle East and Muslim-populated countries in Asia support and fund these schools. In Nigeria, the recruitment of would- be terrorists goes on subtly underground. It is not only the clerics that use the tactics of propagating conspiracy theories to recruit new Muslim converts and would-be terrorists but also politicians. The irony is that some these educated extremists have their children schooling in Europe and the United States. They also live Western life-styles including living in expensive homes. They use the rhetoric and sometimes the videos of conspiracies such as "The West and Double-Speak" and the Illuminati theories to deceive, brainwash, and motivate the unemployed youths to take arms in the name of jihad against the infidels.

In Nigeria, like the rest of the world, there are in the majority - peace-loving Muslims. Their voices are not reflected in the media. Some of their demonstrations against Jihadists amidst them do not likely get the attention the deadly extremists receive in the media. However, like anything that is destructive and gains easy attention, the bad tends to dominate.

But, for this majority to show that they are in control of defending the name and image of Islam, they must not allow the few to be dictating and directing the discourse about a peaceful religion. To show tolerance of other religions and those that practice those other religion, they must show that they are part of the solution to the terrorists and their destruction of the lives of "infidels." They must intervene when these videos and rhetoric against other religion are being played and circulated by the clerics and some Muslims that appear to be moderate, yet clandestinely propagate hate and destruction because their religion is under attack. They must ensure that fund-raising and infiltration of money into schools that teach extreme religious faith do not exist in their communities. These schools exist, but also they have supporters. In the media, some that believe in the conspiracy theories have access to writing expressing their opinions. For example in the month of May 2013, when Boko Haram has already killed more than

3,600 Nigerians and foreigners (Europeans, Americans, Asians, and Lebanese); the same week two British of Nigerian parents, Michael Adebowale, 22, and Michael Olumide Adebolajo, 28, attacked a 25-year-old British soldier Lee Rigby with knives and a meat cleaver on the open street outside the Woolwich army barracks in southeast London. Commenting on the incident in Nigeria newspaper, Femi Kani–Kayode remarked:

> "Was this whole thing (referring Woolwich incident) to some kind of state-sponsored ¬ Illuminati-style human sacrifice? Was it designed and orchestrated creating more terror in the land and to give them the opportunity to introduce new laws that are draconian, curb immigration and do away with even more civil   liberties on the grounds that they wish to fight the terror?" [11]

Fani-Kayode, a Christian, asked readers, if anyone doubts his assertion that they ought to do themselves a favor and watch David Icke's revealing documentary titled "9/11- It was an Inside Job". It is on YouTube, he said. He also urged readers to find Icke's many books and watch his various documentaries on the murder of Princess Diana. Their worldview will change dramatically after that he disclosed.

He said it is important to note the two suspects were not just British citizens of Nigerian descent, but were both Muslim converts. That is to say they were both brought up as Christians, and then somewhere along the line, they were converted not just to Islam but also to its most extreme and radical brand of Islam. They, then, became dangerous Islamists, who were prepared to kill for their faith. Fani-Kayode raised a question about how they were indoctrinated, who cultivated them, and took them to this point, and how did they get so bad?

While he asked, "Is all that I have written here far-fetched? You may believe so, but I don't. And neither have I gone mad he remarked." "The devil is real. It has been around for years and those that are part of it operate in the deepest secrecy. Yet even if you do not agree with me on anything that I have said here, the questions that I have raised are legitimate, and they are indeed food for thought"[12]

Fani-Kayode is an attorney. He was in government as a special assistant to the former President of Nigeria, Olusengun Obasanjo before his appointed as Aviation Minister. Therefore, the ethos or credibility of persons of his caliber does get to the unemployed youths waiting to be recruited as extremists in Nigeria. Boko Haram is motivated by this style of rhetoric even as they are at war in Nigeria. Fani-Kayode's article received wide circulation. Boko Haram, even though its name means "Western education is sin" ironically, its members do receive all their messages through western –developed technologies; even from their hiding caves in Niger-Nigeria and Cameroon border hill villages and caves where the Jihadists now hide following assaults by the Joint Military Task Force to destroy the group.

Fani-Kayode comes from the south where he is of Yoruba extract. His former position as a Minister, his family and his Christian background make his statement more credible and appealing to Northern fundamentalists even if he may not recognize the impact of his statements. His statements, he may not realize has more appeals to extremists; this is when compared to similar statements from a Northern Muslim or mullah.

Words spreading of the West (UK and United States) attempts to wipe Islam from the face of the earth are common rhetoric of clerics as well as educated Muslims in Northern Nigeria. The perception of West conspiracy to frame Islam and Muslims in the news is part of resistance by extremists and one major reason they wanted to oppose and if possible destroy anything Western including people in Southern Nigeria that accept "Western" religion and lifestyles.

While majority of Nigerians dismiss the premise being disseminated about the Western power demonizing Islam as unfounded, some conspiracy theories have also emerged about the North using the wealth from the South to develop Northern Nigeria to the disadvantage of the South. The conspiracy theorists believe that the idea has been long planned, and they are waiting, hoping that Nigeria will eventually break apart and the North will escape with wealth derived from South and make Mecca of break-way Northern Nigeria.

There is also a conspiracy theory about Northern elite and politicians as sponsors of terrorism against Christians - particularly against Igbos (Christians) of Southeast Nigeria. Boko Haram, the theorists claim was bred and financed by Northern political elites to make Nigeria ungovernable because a Christian from South, Dr. Goodluck Jonathan was elected the president of Nigeria. The statement by former head of state General Mohamadu Buhari (Rtd.) even though he has denied the making the statement, but it still fuels the theories. However, many Southerners believed that the terrorism on Nigeria soil was part of the Northern elite's agenda to make Nigeria ungovernable for President Jonathan who happens to be a Christian from the South. Northern political and religious leaders have since dismissed these allegations and propaganda disseminated by people wanting to disintegrate Nigeria.

As more Northern Muslims of Fulani descent are now migrating into Southern parts of Nigeria in the name of business of "selling cows," there is a conspiracy theory about the Northern politicians and religious elite responsible for sponsoring the migration of Fulani cattle ranchers to the south. The ranchers are nomads and are believed that their life style may be now a disguise of foot soldiers (Jihadists) ready to strike at any moment of a command. Incidents of Hausa-Fulani cattle ranchers migrating south attacking villagers in the Southeastern states in Nigeria does give credence that these nomads – ranchers could be violent. Their attacks in Benue and some parts of Igbo land in the South with machetes and AK 47 riffles have been on the rise. There were reports of these Fulani nomads mounting illegal checkpoints with the goal of stopping passenger vehicles and robbing passengers. Since the presence of these nomads could not witnessed in every part of Igbo land, the gradually building mosques in the southeastern states of Nigeria built by Southern Muslim converts, and preaching for acceptance of Islam into their communities raises fears that sooner or later, the North may not even need these foot soldiers, as it would be a replication of experiences of "brothers' fighting against one another in the name of "religions" (Islam versus Christianity) that have split them apart.

While there has not been any serious threat to peace by nomads migrating to Southeast Nigeria, there were instances in Benue and Jos – middle belt zone of the country, where the same Nomads were received and over the years, their attempts to control political and religious activities in communities they migrated have put them at odds with their hosts. The conflict has led to death toll of Christians in thou sands because of sectarian violence. Some pundits have warned that the Southern States opening their doors to these Muslim Nomads should be careful before the experiences in Jos, Benue and Adamawa States repeat in the South. In essence, the theory is that these Nomads are not only selling their merchandise-cows as they travel through every Southern States, but they are like foot soldiers - surveyors mapping the routes and location for an eventual Jihadists attack that may be on their long term goal of Islamizing the South. Pundits say that it is just a matter of time, while other disagree that these nomads are following their pattern of lifestyle that dated more than a thousand years.

No matter how one dismisses the conspiracy theorists, Muslim Jihadists migrating to the South in the disguise of "cattle sellers," or ranchers is signaling high security alert to Southerners. Book Haram targets Christians in the North, the Christians in the South are welcoming these Muslim "Jihadists" in the south, buying their cows, and providing them money for their eventual war to Islamize Nigeria according Mazi Obi Ejike, a Christian from Southeast Nigeria. "This is what Igbos in particular cannot tolerate," he emphasized.

As an observer of Nigeria Muslim and Christian relationships Mazi Ejike observed the patronage of the Muslim nomads (cattle sellers) by Christians (Igbos in particular) in the South shows about the dynamic personalities and cultural value of tolerance and acceptance that are inherent in Igbo culture in particular and Nigeria culture in general. This is in spite of love and hate relationship between Muslims and Christians - relationship that most often were determined by politicians and religious leaders based on their personal and selfish political interests.

While the threat of Boko Haram attack in the South is real,

Igbo town organizations met in Enugu in July10, 2014 and warned that Igbos are alert about any infiltration of Boko Haram suspects into the South. Meanwhile, the arrest of suspected unemployed Northerners in the South particularly, Port Harcourt and Lagos routinely goes on. In a country with free migration and settlements, the lack of identity cards or any social security identification makes the tasks of determining who is a Nigerian or an immigrant from Niger or Chad; and who is a terrorist more daunting and sometimes impossible to dictate

Since the Jihadists initial targets were Igbos of Southeastern Nigeria and Christians (their interests and property), there is no doubt that the fundamentalists have as their priority the weakening of strong-willed people as part of the agenda in the Islamization of Nigeria. The Jihadists envisaged that the Igbos are the strongest in terms of numbers (population that are not Muslims yet). Since the Igbos are strong-willed, and have economic strength, converting them to Islam will be difficult. Therefore, Jihadists weakening their power by force or through pitting them to fight one another will be an easy road to con-quering them.

On another perspective, Boko Haram's perception of Igbos as representative of anything Western is in no doubt cursor to the hatred of Igbos – agenda that is justified by religious bigotry. Unlike the West, where some members of the Yoruba tribe embraced Islam, the Igbos embraced the North through inter-marriages and business rela-tionships, but with very few converting to Islam. Since the Igbos are culturally known for their migration patterns, they consequently adopt other cultures along their migration path, but this has not happened with Hausa or Muslim cultures. For the Igbos, their adoption and assimilation into Hausa cultures and Muslim religion have been very low. Igbos whole-hearted acceptance and affiliation with the Western missionaries (more than Hausa or Muslim cultures) continues to cause disdain of Igbos from some Muslims – extremists in particular and now terrorist group carrying out Jihadists agenda.

These affiliations and developments fit the conspiracy that the Igbos is too embracing to Western cultures and religion (but not Islam), and therefore a "sell-out" to the society especially their extreme-ideological religion with Sharia laws as its backbone. With a claim of affiliation to Israel, the Igbos are regarded as Zionists in character and form. These perceptions run deep across Muslims in Nigeria and around the world. Considering that the Igbos are Christians, and their affiliation with the West dates back to early missionaries in Nigeria, the Igbos represent anything and everything Western.   li

The Igbos, like the Yorubas have high level of Western education, but their tradition and culture have impacted by Western cultures unlike the Yorubas and other tribes in Nigeria. Therefore, targeting the Igbos as prospects for convert to Islam has more to do with Jihadists agenda than other reasons. However, tribalism and prejudice against Igbos' entrepreneurship, coupled with Igbos identification, culturally with Judaism opens them to discrimination. Christianity is viewed by an average Muslim as "Western" culture. In essence, Igbos identification with Western cultures and values establish reasons why the Igbos are targeted by fundamentalists, and now Boko Haram. These reasons are a combination of myths, and some evidence that scholars have explored and produced books, films and documentaries to support Igbos identity to Judaism.

While myths and conspiracy theories dominate debate on issues of importance that have socio-political implications for Nigeria.

What the average Nigerians say on the streets about issues on the global news cycle such as Boko Haram are essential to understanding why some experts claimed that the rhetoric of politicians and clerics are some of the leading voices in the propaganda against the West. The rhetoric has been on going before 9/11 and the war on terror. The propaganda against the West has gained ground over very long period. The fact that there were no plans or programs to counter the impact of these "brain-washing" messages in Nigeria is shocking to these observers and to a cross section of Nigerians. Opinion polls to measure the feelings of Nigerians about Boko Haram say a lot. The polls revealed these messages against the West and Christianity do affect the "conspiracy theorists" and their messages to win mind of not just Muslims, but Christians, as well. These views are revealing.

On the streets of Abuja, "Boko Haram is allegedly just a name given to the creation of few Northern politicians and elders to fight President Jonathan, whom they see as a Christian from the south that should not rule Nigeria," claims Jide Lawal. "I think that there's more to this Boko Haram nuisance than meets the eye," said Bello, a resident of Abuja.

While the Northern elders are blamed for the founding and sustenance of Boko Haram, some interviewees blame the West as sponsors of Boko Haram. Some believe that the West even formulated the name. According to Zakari, a commuter in the city of Kano, one of the hubs of Islamic centers in Nigeria. "When it comes to the West, do not believe anything. I am suspecting that there are Western hands in the group." He backs up his argument with the conspiracy theorists that believe that while African leaders go to the West, sit and dine with Westerners, these people (West) sit down and plan years ahead of what they want to do or see happen not just in Africa but around the world." He continued, "I see the Western hand in Boko Haram since they have predicted that Nigeria will be a failed state by 2015." Like Jide, Zakari explains, "the problem with the West is that they could never be trusted. Yes, the American People, the Europeans…on a person to person level, they are good people…..but when it comes to their countries or their national interests, it is like the more they look into your eyes, the more lies you hear. They are very smart and have projections of what they want happen in 20 years not just in their countries but in Africa." He concludes that what happens in Africa and also in Nigeria regarding Western support for Boko Haram and their denial that they are helping Nigeria fight the insurgents is like the hand of Esau but the voice of Jacob in the Bible" exclaimed Bosco Oshodi. "Exactly! Unfortunately, we have very willing tools in the North due to poverty and illiteracy."

"The Oyibos (meaning the West in native dialect) have never meant well for the Black man. They feel they are superior to us in every way so when they see us rising, they do everything to suppress us," said Ibrahim. On the claim of Western influence and domination – all geared to subdue Africans, some of the interviewees dismissed the claim. One respondent said. "No, I don't agree with the assertion that the West is out there to destroy the black man." He continued, "Do some soul-searching and just take a look to the leadership or the governance in Nigeria.

Take for example since independence… What have we achieved? We are busy maiming and killing ourselves; some politicians are robbing the country and yet we are comfortably playing the blame game. I do not care what anybody says, but let the truth be told, the buck stops here." He concludes, why are we complaining, after all, we were made by the same creator of other races. God ...he gave us the same brain and same 24 hours in a day, so what are we talking about?"

In dismissing that the West is against the Black man, another interviewee said, "Why are we complaining? How come China has become great even when the West never liked China and their people to grow at anything including competition?" The West never liked them too. What about Japan and South Korea? Japan cannot halt their production of Toyota to allow Kia to penetrate the market. China is already a great economic power because they looked inwards. So what stops Nigeria from using her abundant resources to become great?" asked Joshua. "It's like God's apprentices made us," replied Biola. This elicited laughter. Said Ibrahim: "Ajaokuta Steel Company is an example. It was meant to be the largest in Africa. "Then corruption happened!" interjected Joshua. "Well, it was a conspiracy by the West. Ajaokuta Steel Limited was to enable us to become makers and exporters of steel.[13]

The Russians were awarded the contract because the West did not like the idea, they started the project, suddenly the West became interested and was awarded the civil engineering work, and then the cold war started. The West used their civil engineering companies to frustrate the project. Africa is the largest market for Western automobiles, so if Nigeria begins to produce steel, they will lose the market and that was why they conspired to slow the growth of the project," said Ibrahim. "Ah, your school fees were not in vain. You're making sense," joked Biola.

"So you now see why the Boko Haram thing can as well be a conspiracy? Nigeria is blessed in every sense of the word, and if it is allowed to develop will become a big threat to the West and so the best thing is to destabilize her, not from outside but from within; set them up against themselves and fragment the country, Joshua remarked.[14]

Joshua explained that it is not just the West, Arabs and Nigerians are aiding in the destruction of the country that took life and death for Nigeria's fathers of Independence to build. He remarked, "Kano, Jos and Kaduna would have been strong business corridors, but look at what has happened! According to him an average Nigerian will prefer to get N1million as his own share even if the country will lose N10 million ($62, 112) in the process. "It is that bad. I know of a Lebanese business-man owing the domestic power supply company in Nigeria - Power Holding Company of Nigeria (PHCN) N50, 000 (about $310) but was willing to bribe them with N40, 000 ($248) instead of paying the N50, 000 and getting a receipt." He expressed disappointment with the system with laws that are not followed or enforced. He responded, "This is aiding a foreigner to defraud us. Will a White guy allow a Black man to defraud his government?" asked Sani. "Impossible,"[15]

These conversations tell one thing that even though the majority of Nigerians, mainly Southern youth would like to migrate to the United States as Pew Survey revealed, the sentiments that often are created against the West runs deep among Southerners. These conspiracy theories as alleged are often given attention and propagated by both Muslim and Christian elites mainly politicians and some religious clerics in the North.

A source told the author how as a teenager and a first year college student in the 90s, he was given a free video depicting the West as unreliable and untruthful. The documentary video titled "Double-Speak" according to the student has been duplicated as many times as possible and distributed to both Muslim and Christian youth. The lessons in the videos were propaganda tailored to persuade viewers or would–be converts to Islam to be aware of West and their secret "white and bold lies." The videos directed to viewers according to the source is about conspiracy theories and events in the United States that depict the United States as fabricating events to empower and also "rule the world."   While these conspiracy theories exist without any counter information by the State Department at the time, things have since changed in the Arab world with anti-United States counter propaganda machinery, but not that I am aware in Africa. Sources disclosed that programs are on the way to use the media and other communication tools to dissuade youths in Northern Nigeria from their view of the West as "evil." The idea is to build mistrust of the West to viewers, thus spreading the ideas that Islam is pure and religion of truth and only the true and just religion. According to inside sources in Muslim schools, these are lessons that children and teenager in so-called religious schools learn every day. It is the same ideology that its extreme form is guiding Boko Haram and their motivation for strife they are causing not just to Christians but Muslims who do not agree with their ideology.

Boko Haram fighters, before that assumed that name

"Western education is sinful" and started their campaign; the Jihadists have been instructed in their 'religious' schools and they live up to what they have been preached and taught in their Mosques or religious school about the West.

CHAPTER 6

Boko Haram – Why are the Igbos (South-eastern Christians) Easy Targets of Fundamentalists in Nigeria?

Inter-tribal marriages among Muslims and Igbos in Nigeria – do take place, but not a common practice. Marriages are often between top military officers and Igbo women. Hardly are Igbos married to Muslim women for reasons that have more to do with religion that restricts Muslim women to marrying fellow Muslims unlike Igbo culture that is more liberal when it comes to association and who a person marries. However, these marriages to Igbos by Northern Muslims and some politicians have not quelled the love-hate relationship between Muslims and Christians – which at times is very difficult to separate between people, their religion and where they come from. Overall, it all boils to politics and how it is being exploited for reasons that include 'us" and "them" and power control.

Having lived among Muslims, there is no question that majority of Muslims are peace loving people. The same could be said of Islam, a religion with more than one billion people who very few number of followers are exploiting the religion for political selfish goals. In essence, nobody is convinced that what extremists or Jihadists say or do represented the religion or its ten nets.

Nigeria extremists and the problems fundamentalists create are exacerbated by internal and external influences. Former United States

Ambassador to Nigeria, Princeton Lyman highlighted the challenges Nigeria has to deal.[1] Since Nigeria is politically strategic, the use of religion to establish presence and power control could attribute to violence in Nigeria. That these powerful influences do cause frictions is self-denial. Nigeria has to deal with forces inside and outside middling into Nigeria's political and religious affairs to ensure their political and religion is vital and influencing decisions Nigeria makes internally and in global affairs. This is a challenge Nigeria leaders must watch.

Evidences show that Muslims and Christians live amicably together in neighboring African countries without the level of mistrust, prejudice and violence as witnessed in Nigeria. In Ghana and Togo, rarely do Christians and Muslims clash as they do in Nigeria. So why do Muslims and Christians clash in Nigeria? Another question, why are Igbos (Christians) always targets of religious fundamentalists in the North? It is puzzling, but not difficult to find reasons why whenever there is rioting in the Middle East, Palestine or in the streets of Paris or Western capital cities over one controversial Islamic issue or the other – either with the West or the Israelis, the Igbos are targeted in Nigeria's Northern States? – an anonymous Nigerian (not of Igbo tribe) asked. A typical example was the political unrest that rocked Egypt when Morsi's was ousted in July 3, 2013 through a "military coup" after massive protests against him. When he was removed from office, the Muslim Brotherhood demonstrated wanting the military to restore Morsi to power.[2] As with other political and religious incidents that have taken place in Muslim world and have their ripple effects in Nigeria - more than 4000 Muslims youth rallied in northern Nigeria in solidarity with Muslim Brotherhood demanding the return of Egypt's Islamist former president Mohamed Morsi, ousted by the military.[3] These events are not far to explain the role religion plays in politics in Northern Nigeria and affiliation of Muslims and Islamic groups to North Africa, the Middle East and elsewhere in the world. The reality is that most of these events that cause rioting and the often attacks on Igbos and their property have nothing to do with religion, rather settling political old-grudges for no reasons other than jealousy, prejudice, and tribalism that religion is an undercover to put out those human gullibilities.

Politics may also explain some of the reasons why in a secular state such as Nigeria; when issues that are purely political that has nothing to do with religion, when also questioned by Christians, it is perceived as a confrontation to Islam. In most times the reaction to simple question triggers anger and animosity, leading to violence and bloodbath on the streets. However, considering that Nigeria in the North has countries that are Muslim nations and with Nigeria's open boundaries, extremists from neighboring countries have easily infiltrated into Nigeria through these unsecured borders. Nigeria easily attracts extremists and clerics from neighboring countries that freely migrate to support Jihadists' movement and join in the "holy war."[4]

Nigeria is the most populated country in Africa. Nigeria's strategic position in Africa and the world makes the country a magnet to interests that include political and religious power players. It is also an economic powerhouse of the region, and Africa's largest economy. These are both Nigeria's strengths that are attractive to political power players for control and manipulations. With internal security threats by those exploiting her diversity to cause trouble instead of concentrating on beneficial policies, Nigeria's attention is diverted to defending itself from detractors when the focus should be how to defend itself from external enemies, focus on programs that will improve the lives of her people while strategizing to gain investors to develop her economy. These threats from within and external environments also come in the form of tribal and religious violence. Executors, who come in different styles and forms as non-Nigerians can migrate to the country without identification, they wear robes of brotherhood, easily absorbed into the system, using religion as a disguise to destabilize Nigeria.

There are other reasons why Igbos are targets of extremists. The Igbos, often victims of these attacks are stereotyped as "the Jews of Africa." No studies showed whether those affiliations have played any role in the ethnic targeting of Igbos in the name of religious riots that sometimes-Western policy on Middle East or perceived as anti-Islamic by fundamentalists often trigger riots excavating to massacre of the Igbos.

Speaking before the British Parliament in April 2013, former Governor of Abia State, Chief Orji Kalu disclosed that the Igbos have suffered in Nigeria, Kalu recalled the Igbo massacres in Kano, in 1980; Maiduguri, in 1982; Yola, in 1984; Gombe, in 1985; Kaduna, in 1986; Bauchi, in 1991; Funtua, in 1993; Kano, in 1994; Damboa, in 2000 and the April 6 massacre, in 2005. He said that although the number of Igbos slaughtered by Boko Haram was yet to be documented, there could be no question that a disproportionate percentage of the thousands of victims, dead, maimed, or permanently impoverished, comprise Igbo people.

According to him, "Nigerian fundamentalists who had been

provoked not by any direct misconduct by the Igbos, but perhaps, because, Prophet Mohammed was blasphemed in Denmark by an European artist or because Allah's name was "used in vain" in Los Angeles by an American satirist, have killed Igbo. He said that it was in order to address some of the issues that *Njiko Igbo*, a pan-Igbo group was formed. [5]

This notion of connecting Igbos to the Jewish people of Israel could also be traced to the tenets of the Hamitic hypothesis which posited that certain superior groups and tribes came from northeast Africa or beyond including Israel and survived in sub-Saharan Africa.[6] Horton was absorbed to the idea that "The Igbo tribe could trace their origins back to the "Lost Tribes of Israel," and that the Igbo language was heavily influenced by Hebrew."[7]

George Basden, who first arrived in Igbo territory in 1900, confirmed the claim by scholars of Igbos' Jewish heritage. Baden, a scholar and an ethnographer is recognized as a leading expert on the subject of Igbos and their Jewish origin.[8] Elizabeth Isichei offered insights into the origin and history of Igbo people. [9] Olaudah Equiano's biography described the analogies between Jewish customs, law, belief and those of Igbos.[10] John Ogilby account revealed there were indeed Jews and Jewish or Israeli customs in West Africa; which Tudor Parfitt, affirmed that Jewish customs were to be found in the Igbo areas of West Africa. "To this day, for some Igbos, the idea that "Igbo" and

"Hebrew" (or ivri) are one and the same word and that   the two languages are closely related is quite widespread."[11]

Former Premier of Eastern Nigeria, Dr. Michael Okpara, and a renowned Igbo leader was accused of declaring himself "an Israeli" during the Biafra war that coincided with the six-day Arab-Israeli conflict of June 1967. The "Biafra War" was read as North-South confrontation, same as the Arab-Israeli war. Whether any evidence supports the comparison remains to be found. It is also yet to be established that the Jews actually helped Igbos during the civil war.

In the 21st century, Igbos are perceived as the "Jews of Africa" for various reasons. Igbos success in business and politics is often compared to Jews. They two (Igbos and Jews) have similar qualities to assimilate easily wherever they find themselves and do well in business and in their careers. With a small homeland, they often gain economic success through ingenious efforts, money that they repatriate to develop their homeland. Original owners of the land where Igbos migrate are often feeling sense of anxiety, discomfort and uncomfortable with "these immigrants" and their economic success. With the evidence that reveals Igbos migrate to their "lands" and quickly gain economic control does increase prejudice. Igbos' boasted dynamism in adapting to their new environment and sometimes-dominating businesses in their new homeland makes the Igbos suspects, thus leading to tensions between Igbos and their hosts. An example of Igbos' ingenious survival instinct was at the end of Nigeria civil war (July 6, 1967 – January 15, 1970).

The Nigeria Civil War, also known as the Nigeria-Biafra war took place because of failed attempted secession of the southeastern provinces of Nigeria as the self-proclaimed Republic of Biafra. At the end of the civil war, every Igbo man was only allowed by law to withdraw only $25 pounds (even when the person has over $1 million pounds in that same bank account) as part of the "reconciliation" program. The Igbos in spite of the setback has rebounded economically. They did this through their individual effort and group's self-determination. The strength of the Igbos does not go well with the other tribes especially in the Muslim North where rural nomadic lifestyle and agriculture are ways of life. The courage of the Igbos and their entrepreneurship exacerbate further prejudice and the discrimination.

For some states in the South that have established networks and collaborations with the Jewish state of Israel, including organized annual pilgrimages to the Holy Land, business travels, agricultural and educational exchange programs do not improve Igbos relationship with Muslims whose religious and economic relationships are tied to Arabs, Saudi Arabia and North Africa. "Many observers believe that the Ibos' high level of education, coupled with the extremely high number of managerial and professional posts they occupied, generated intense envy among some Nigerians." Jeffrey D. Blum was reporting on the visit US State Department six-man fact-finding mission in 1969 to examine the needs of both Nigeria and Biafra and to make recommendations to the U.S. government about the necessary forms and amount of possible aid to reduce hunger that was used by the Nigeria side of the war against Biafra. Senator Charles E. Goodell (R.-N.Y.), was the head of the delegation while his administrative assistant Charles W. Dunn was in charge of the mission's diplomatic aspects.[12]

The present situation at the Gaza Strip with the unfortunate killings of young Palestinians, the expanding Israeli occupation of Palestinian land and the threat of war with Iran, the movie trailer or cartoon of Islamic leader in faraway countries of Middle East, United States and Europe do also help build positive relationships with Muslims. It is this loophole in the process that Jihadists exploit. These events cause reactions in Nigeria from extremists that target Igbos whenever rioting breaks out in Europe and the Middle East.

The growing population of Igbo Jews of Nigeria - known as the "Beneiv-Yisrael," who claimed they traced their origin from the biblical tribes of Gad, Asher, Dan, and Naphtali does not build friendship with jihadists. These Igbos traced their migration through Syria, Portugal and Libya into West Africa around 740 C.E. to Nigeria. They claimed that they were joined by more Jewish immigrants from Portugal and Libya in 1484 and 1667 respectively.[13]

These claims and the counter arguments notwithstanding, the British colonial powers preference to hand over the premiership of Nigeria to the North after Nigeria's independence in 1960. Christianity remains a bond between the West and Nigerians in the South while Islam remains a very strong bond between the North and Arabs in Africa and Middle East. The travels and evangelization trips by missionaries dating back to more than two centuries bring uncertainties and mistrust between Muslims and Christians. While Muslims head to the North to Saudi Arabia, the South (mainly Igbos) head to Israel for their pilgrimages.

For the extremists (fundamentalists) in the North who are never short of expressing their goals, disdain for West, and unapologetic for "holy war" to spread their ideologies beyond their Northern borders, these connections to Israel by the Igbos are perceived as threats, thus, on any account or incident of provocation, whether relevant to Islamization agenda or not, Igbos are easily targeted by fundamentalists – as their disdain of Western culture and values; and becomes an opportunity to gain publicity, recruit new members at the expense of deaths of the Igbos..

When these fundamentalists perceived that their religion is under attack or threats by the West through policies or through media framing of Islam and Muslims, the fundamentalists often find easy target to avenge those anger and frustrations, and Igbos mainly living in the North (since Igbos like the Jews are migrants and the Igbos perceived association with the Jews) become easy targets. Fundamentalists' agenda are always manifested on TV, rallies, and even so-called "religious events" where they reveal their disenchantment with the West and Israel. The fundamentalists are also against the secularity of Nigeria states they perceive as "unholy," therefore, a "Holy War" would purify the country from influences of the West. Fundamentalist's' unrelenting goal is to resist any values that corruption their culture as they find convenient using Sharia to back up their arguments.

Nigeria's fundamentalists no doubt share the same ideologies with their peers around the world, in particular Arab and Middle East countries where extreme religious beliefs have torn countries apart. In Nigeria's situation, such attempts have persisted, however, authorities and Nigerians have resisted the fundamentalists from using religion to achieve their other objectives of destroying the country by introducing extreme theocracy or sharia laws.

Boko Haram (Western education is sin) currently operating in Nigeria is a mutation of fundamentalist groups from the past trying to achieve Jihadists goals with new name, new technology and global collaboration from Al-Qaeda network around the Mediterranean, Middle East and Somalia. They walk from the sidelines into the political center stage, using religion as a front to achieve their political goals, even as they take anti-religion and anti-Christian actions such as suicide bombings using teenage boys and girls to do so; kidnapping of Chibok schoolgirls from their dormitories and beheading male high school students with machetes because they were Christians. One thing that fundamentalists want to do is instill fears into all of us. Jihadists also want to play big role to push their agenda (politics, not religion) through at costs that may hurt and haunt others. Another feature fundamentalists share is fear of any kind of change, especially in modern as she advances from traditional society to a modern secular nation.

CHAPTER 7

Boko Haram – Negotiating Amnesty Amidst Spiraling Violence & Deaths.

When on July 29, 2009, the designated Boko Haram's leader Mohammed Yusuf died while in police custody, his immediate successor Abubakar Shekau went underground for a while after escaping from the gun battle with security agents that led to the capture of Yusuf in his father-in-law's goat pen in Maiduguri. During the encounter leading to the arrest of Mohammed Yusuf, more than 500 people were killed – most of the victims were civilians. The death of Boko Haram's members in the clash was at least a success that the Nigeria security forces were quick to acknowledge their "successful' operation. However, the victory did not stop Boko Haram assaults and suicide bombings, but rather intensified the spiraling violence committed by the Jihadists in the North and Central states of Nigeria by the terror group.

Since the July 29, 2009 clash with security forces, Boko Haram has carried out a series of attacks including gun battles with security agents and suicide bombings of civilian targets. Its military and guerilla tactics included suicide bombings of Christian churches including fellowship centers located inside Military Barracks. Haram fighters have also attacked motor parks and Sabon Gari, where mostly Igbos converge in large numbers for business and leisure were attacked. Members of the security forces (military, police and State Secrete Services) were also attacked. They included police stations, police check points, immigration, and prisons. Other targets were elementary schools, high schools, universities, newspaper offices, and the United Nations building in Abuja that housed more than 26 agencies of the international organization. Similarly, Boko Haram has attacked "infidels," and Muslims, clerics, traditional leaders, and politicians from the North who criticized its ideology or tactics and were perceived to be collaborating with the state to identify and arrest Boko Haram fighters. A handful of foreigners were also kidnapped, in particular in the months of January and July 2012.[1] Prior to these incidents, Boko Haram's leader had appeared in many videos posted online claiming responsibility for the majority of attacks and threatening future violence.

Overall, more than 60 police stations and military facilities in 10 Northern and Central States in Nigeria have been attacked. Between June 7, 2011 and January 17, 2012, more than 142 Christians were killed inside churches while victims worshipped. The attacks took place in 18 churches and were carried out by armed gunmen and suicide bombers across eight Northern and Central States. Between January 8 and September 2012, Boko Haram killed about 119 police (of 211 military and police officers killed). At the same period, Boko Haram carried out more than 20 major attacks and 50 smaller assaults in the city of Kano state alone. These numbers represented, overall, the number of attacks by the Jihadists in the country in 2010 and 2011 combined.[2]

A Boko Haram member told reporters that the Jihadists were on a revenge mission in retaliation for its members killed by security forces on July 29, 2009 operation that led to clashes with the sect members.[3] Six members of the sect on trial for the November 2011 suicide bombing of a Catholic Church in Suleija revealed Boko Haram's plans for their sustained attacks and suicide missions in Nigeria. One of the members of the sect told the court that they were avenging the death of its leader Yusuf at the hands of the security agents, [4] thus their attack on churches. Boko Haram's spokesman, Abu Qada, remarked, "There will never be peace until our demands were met".[5]

The group's objectives included making Nigeria a failed State like Somalia while imposing a strict Islamic culture on the entire Nigeria region ruled under fundamentalists' sharia laws to ensure that it can use the country as a base to reach Western targets in Europe and the United States. Boko Haram has carried these threats with attacks leading to deaths of more than 12,000 people, Nigerians and foreigners alike. While engaging in gun attacks and suicide bombings, its tactics also include kidnapping Christians, taking them to their camps, and forcing them to convert to Islam. Those that refused to convert have been strangled or shot in the back of their head.[6]

Even with a State of Emergency declared by President Jonathan Goodluck, and a strong military offensive against Boko Haram insurgents mounted by the Joint Military Task Force, the insurgents seemed undeterred in their attacks on new targets. Motor parks where Igbos converge to board for road travel to the East have been targeted; buses carrying passengers mainly Christians travelling to Eastern Nigeria have been attacked at gas stations while stopped to gas their vehicles. Other venues of attacks include police checking points, police stations, prison facilities where prisoners were freed and wardens shot to death; and immigration checkpoints, universities, elementary and high schools were not spared. Media houses and United Nations buildings were not exempted from attacks resulting in a high number of casualties.

Amidst the persistent attacks even as the Joint Military Task Force drafted more than 2000 military personnel to quell the insurgents following the Presidential State of Emergency declared on December 31, 2011 in three Northern States of Adamawa, Borno and Yobe, a cross section of Nigerians were still not pleased with the administration's efforts. As Boko Haram gets more sophisticated in averting the military going after the terrorists, some accused the Joint Military Task Force as incompetent even though it comprised some of Nigeria's best military personnel; others believed that some renegades and supporters of Boko Haram within the military and the administration might be undermining the mission to destroy the terrorists.

Therefore, with the call for government to protect the lives of its citizens and put an end to the spiraling violence, the office of the president that was not initially opened to dialogue with Boko Haram, but seemed at a point to be listening to people calling for amnesty for the Jihadists. The majority of the advocates for amnesty were Northern traditional and religious leaders. Nevertheless, the attention to advocates of amnesty did not stop President Jonathan Goodluck from suspending the constitutional guarantees of the 15 towns and cities in the North and Central Nigeria under the six-month state of emergency. Still the State of Emergency did not improve the security situation in these states. However, it was gathered that the president, known to be a good listener, later rejected the call for the amnesty. According to *Human Rights Watch* Report, "Boko Haram carried out more attacks and killed more people during the six months than all of 2010 and 2011 combined." [7]

Nigerians have received mixed signals on actions by their president to address Boko Haram's threats to national security. They have wondered if the problem the military and police were encountering in not gaining tactical and military advantage over Boko Haram fighters were because of lack of military personnel training, equipment or the mistrust of members of the security agencies of their commander –in-chief. Some wondered whether the indictment of some of his cabinet members or Northern leaders sympathizing with Boko Haram may have cost him the royalty of his men and women at the forefront on the fight to eliminate Boko Haram threats. All the same, a statement to reiterate president's claims about some members of his cabinet are supporters of the terrorists was independently confirmed by Chief of Army Staff (COAS), Lieutenant General Azubuike Ihejirika. He disclosed that some soldiers have been interacting with Boko Haram insurgents and divulging vital secrets of the military operations. [8]

The Federal government has admitted that the security agents were not trained to face the type of threats posed by Boko Haram and its gorilla-styled warfare. However, the resilience of the terrorists led to speculations by cross section of Nigerians that the composition of the terrorist leadership, and its organizational structure was more than the military could combat. Before Boko Haram emerged, Nigerians have accused their military of lacking in preparedness as they (military personnel) have become involved in politics and lacked focus. With Boko Haram, the fears that the military is facing gorilla-kind of warfare that the military are not used to makes the mistrust Nigerians have of their military experience to dislodge Boko Haram more believable. Boko Haram on their part has taken advantage of this military weakness to attack and disappear within the public. These criticisms of the military readiness to confront Boko Haram Jihadists persisted even as there were evidences to support that Nigeria military has led peace mission that liberated Liberia and Sierra Leone from rebels and restored democracy in these countries. They have also participated successfully in UN peace mission across the world.

With links to Al-Qaeda in the Middle East and in the Islamic Maghreb in the Mediterranean, majority of Nigerians feared that Nigeria might be heading to same unending terrorist attacks on civilian population as Al-Qaeda and its affiliates in Afghanistan, Pakistan and Iraq have done. Even at that, evidence that the United States leading the Coalition Forces in Afghanistan found it difficult to quell the terrorists with advanced military training, weapons, superb intelligence, huge financial investment and the war against terror seemed not yet won; raises the fear that Nigeria may not survive Boko Haram's violence.

The Joint Military Force set up by President Jonathan has achieved tremendous success, even though the security agents were accused of high-handedness and execution of Boko Haram suspects without trial.[9] Therefore, the belief that Boko Haram is overrunning Nigeria security agencies and agents and winning on the war against Boko Haram and terrorism may be subjective evaluation of the situation depending on who makes the judgment. However, security forces have from eye witness account reduced all the anxieties about their ability. They have displayed tactical skills, determination and unrelenting efforts in their pursuit to dislodge the terrorists.

Nevertheless, evidences revealed Boko Haram has also scored repeated and successful assults on its targets even with state of emergency and curfew declared in North and Central States in Nigeria. All the same, the overwhelming pursuit of Boko Haram by Nigeria security agents and the terrorists fleeing their camps to escape to neighboring countries in Niger, Mali and Cameroon suggests the terrorists are on the run. This is as news of more attacks and casualties from Boko Haram recent attacks in Nigeria and its neighboring border villages in Cameroon and Chad has shown a rise in these attacks.

The news that Mohammad toppled Boko Haram's leader Sheikh Abubakar Shekau was discovered not to be true. However, while the news of his death was circulating, it was gathered that Nigeria's government entered closed-doors negotiation with the a faction of Boko Haram terrorists for an elusive peace to the conflict that has claimed many lives since 2009.[10] Again, another aberration to the story about Boko Haram and government handling of communication to beat the terrorists propaganda network.

While it is not clear how the peace negotiation will eventually work and be sustained, evidence from captured ammunitions and documents from Boko Haram's camps and hideouts during raids by the Joint Military Task Force confirmed that the group has international affiliations. Identities of non-Nigerians were also found at camps and building used by Boko Haram for its operations in Maiduguri.

In essence, Boko Haram has advanced into cell-based organizations that are unified under the control of its current leader, Shekau.[11] Therefore, it is not known which faction will lay down arms in case there is a negotiation and which of the cells that will continue attacks on its targets. This concern becomes more troubling amidst several underlying factors that may signal weakening sovereign state in Nigeria despite the intensify efforts by the Federal Government to dislodge or eradicate Boko Haram. Pundits have predicted without the Federal government addressing tactically economic, socio political, failing education standards, digital divide, and religious (using the same might and determination that it has pursued Jihadists in addressing Nigeria's other problems, they (pundits) warned that it is a matter of time before another militant rises from another part of the country (in addition to others that are existing, but not active).

Meanwhile, the level of unemployment across Nigeria and, in particular, the North continues to skyrocket. The situation does not help in the war on terror authorities to capture insurgents and quell the violence. As a hungry man is an angry man, the poor witnessing their leaders living in extreme extravagance – in opulence while the majority of the people cannot afford daily meals has its own downside including posing serious threats to the state. The situation does not help reduce violence as criminal gangs and political thugs soon joined in the violence.

These 'thugs and gangs' – majority of them unemployed youth, do commit some of the attacks attributed to Boko Haram. "Complicating the matter are criminal gangs in the north, including political thugs that are suspected of committing crimes under the guise of Boko Haram."[12] Coupled with poor governance and corruption in Nigeria, some of the critics of Boko Haram, even among Christians wished that the Boko Haram would target elites and political leaders rather than Christians or innocent people. This is in spite of Boko Haram's attacks shaking the citizens' psyche, the cord of multi-cultural and tribal relationships, and increasing tensions between the North (Muslims) and South (Christians). These cross-sections of Nigerians wonder whether the government will be able to dislodge a cell-based and highly structured organization like the Boko Haram.

Since the responsibilities of government to protect its citizens were fading and hope seemed lost; there were divided opinions as to the solution to the internal security problems posed by Boko Haram (with its affiliated terror group the Al-Qaeda). As Boko Haram insurgents were targeting Christians, innocent Nigerians including Muslims that disagreed with their extreme forms of sharia, and foreign workers mainly working in construction sites, hospitals, and schools in the North, the desperation to put an end to the violence became the most pressing problem in every Nigerian's mind.

In the North, views advocating amnesty for Boko Haram fighters represented in the media were of religious, traditional, and political leaders in the North. These leaders supported the granting of amnesty to Boko Haram members in exchange for a truce. The dominant opinion in the south, however, was the opposite. As majority of the victims – the targets of Boko Haram were Christians and Igbos from the Southeastern Nigeria, the voices from this region supported the arrest and immediate trial with death penalty for members of the terror group found guilty of the terror crimes that have taken more than 12,000 lives.

However, amidst the divided opinions, the reality on the ground was that nothing seemed to be working. Boko Haram continues its viral attacks taking lives in hundreds every month. Between the months of January and March 2014, it was reported that Boko Haram killed more than 1, 500 people[13] This was at the time the world was focused on Russian and Ukraine tensions where about 77 people were reported killed during the protest to ousted President Viktor F. Yanukovych.[14]

While evidence showed that the Joint Military Task Force had performed their best in pursuing and killing most members of Boko Haram, the use of the force to quell the insurgent seemed have worked as planned. The use of force attracted criticism from Human Rights Watch and the US government. They condemned the accidental deaths of innocent people and the high-handedness of suspects and extra judicial killings by security agents.

Whereas some in the North perceived the use of force to stop the violence as killing more citizens than the members of Boko Haram, international organizations such as the United Nations stressed that Nigeria's Joint Military Task Force against Boko Haram must thread with caution; observe human rights of citizen to stay away from unnecessary use of force and killings. Secretary General, Ban Ki-Moon, who was reacting to Boko Haram violence in Nigeria and the state of emergency declared by President Goodluck Jonathan, condemned the terrorists, but stressed the need for all concerned to fully respect human rights and safeguard the lives of Nigerians.[15]

Human Rights Watch, U.S. top officials, including the Secretary of State, Senator John Kerry, weighed in calling on Nigerians to guarantee that innocent lives were protected. They called for caution in the use of force by the security agents against Boko Haram. Since the security agents' treatment of detainees, including Boko Haram fighters did not meet international standards as alleged by Human Rights

Watch, evidence suggested that Jihadists never respected the human rights of suspects.

However, majority of Nigerians were less concerned about how Boko Haram members arrested by security agents were treated. Opinions held that the Jihadists deserved no better treatment for killing innocent people in their private homes and in their places of worship churches. Nigerians were more concerned with authorities stopping Boko Haram's attacks and sympathized with thousands of people killed by terrorists and others disabled for the rest of their lives from these attacks. Critics disclosed that these people were often missed in this discourse on terrorists and whether amnesty should be granted to Boko Haram fighters.

While these concerns were raised, the precarious situation of Jihadists targeting Christians and Igbos in particular, polarizes the nation along ethnic and religious lines. The Igbos seek for answers from government about plans to protect the Igbos and their property to avoid ethnic cleansing that may be Boko Haram motivated, but could also include other extremists capturing the tensed situation to attack the Igbos. Some have called for intensified military onslaught against the Jihadists; others called for truce and amnesty. Divided opinions dominated the news with the South (Christians) against amnesty, while Northern leaders supported amnesty. Unfortunately, none presented viable lasting solutions to the problem of terrorism in Nigeria and West African region.

Since January 29, 2009, Boko Haram had maimed and killed more than 12, 000, but it was not clear whether the United States interest and military presence in the region to eliminate the terror from

Al-Qaeda in Maghreb (AQIM) was responsible for the Northern elders calling for amnesty for the terror group. The U.S. located Drone center in Niger (very close to Maiduguri) under the African Military Force – US/African Union security collaboration, but the center did not start operation until the Jihadist in Mali took over the democratically elected government. Through French intervention, the insurgents were defeated, government was restored, but the jihadists fled to neighboring states including Nigeria.

Therefore, it was unknown whether the call for truce and amnesty for Boko Haram terrorists from majority Muslim leaders in the North was necessitated by the fears that displaced insurgents in Mali may invading their territory to cause harm to the institution that these leaders relish for centuries and wanted to prevent any threats to the status quo. It was also alleged that the call for amnesty was motivated by the anxiety over the proximity of the US Drone center in Chad (Niger), located very close to Maiduguri in Northern Nigeria.

Overall, what was worrisome to the leaders in the North was that drones with their reported statistics of casualties from Drone attacks in Afghanistan and Pakistan, the use of any un-manned advance aerial technology in their spaces was not the best option to fighting the insurgents. In short, Drone option for fighting the insurgents was ruled out completely. Some Christians from the South) supported the idea that no Drones should be allowed into Nigeria's airspace as both groups agreed that the technology is not a tool to fight insurgents within residential populated villages and towns. Insurgents who like gorillas attack their targets and filter into the population would expose the civilian population to risks if drones were deployed. With guerilla-tactics of urban fight, victims from drone attacks as witnessed in Afghanistan and Pakistan were innocent civilians, opponents against the use of Drones postulated.

Other reason why Northern elders opposed the use of drones was that they (leaders) were afraid of the reactions of their citizens when Drones go into operation, and risked killing innocent citizens. Nevertheless, those anxieties were more than the terror visited on citizens by Boko Haram experts explain. However, as pundits have observed, Boko Haram, the displaced insurgents from Mali Jihadists-motivated coup d'état, Libya insurgents after the fall of Mummer Gadhafi (some of the displaced Jihadists) and the drones – all are threats to the institution of traditional and religious leaders in the North that they want to protect. These experts disclosed that Northern leaders did not want part of any Drone program to fight insurgents. Furthermore, the use of drones threatens the internal security of Nigeria they also argued. The latter, even among Christians is perceived as a reality that they do not want part of the Drones in Nigeria airspace in the name of fighting terrorists.

As witnessed from the testimonials of leaders and other on the controversial issue of amnesty, majority of the pro-amnesty were traditional, religious and political leaders. Leaders from the south who supported amnesty were people who had long business, social, and some other forms relationships with leaders from the North. With their relationships to Northern leaders, critics explained politics and their selfish interests might have been the motivation for supporting amnesty for Jihadist. In essence, majority of the leaders from the south (Christians) who advocated amnesty for Boko Haram fighters were not sincere.

Critics' anger and frustrations were that majority of the leaders from the North and South advocating for amnesty never considered the plights of victims of Boko Haram suicide bombers. Westerners including civil rights leader, Rev. Jesse Jackson, US Bureau of African Affairs' spokesperson, Ms. Hilary Renner, and Former US President, Bill Clinton had called for an end to the precarious security situation in Nigeria. They appealed to the president to granting amnesty to Boko Haram. However, majority of Nigerians were disappointed by such appeal for amnesty for deadly terrorist group that has killed children and mothers, even in their places of worship on Easter and Christmas church services. Nigerians were afraid that these American leaders must have based their comments on flawed knowledge of events on the ground in the North and may be they based their opinion on messages they were fed by leaders in Northern Nigeria and others in the South asking for amnesty on behalf of Jihadist fighters. That Boko Haram "Jihadists" should be perceived as youth advocating for unemployment in the North, they warned is deceptive.

Speaking at an award ceremony in Abeokuta, Ogun State Nigeria, Bill Clinton had remarked that poverty eradication, education, equitable distribution of wealth and job creation programs for the teeming unemployed graduates in Nigeria could help minimize violence. He said that Nigeria would do better if her leaders efficiently managed her resources. "You have to somehow bring economic opportunity to the people who don't have it.....You have all these political problems — and now violence — that appear to be rooted in religious differences and all the rhetoric of the Boko Harams and others. " [16]

In Nigeria, opinion expressed by Bill Clinton and others were viewed as not helping in the campaign to use force to quell the insurgence in the North and Central states in Nigeria. Critics argued that poverty does not cause insurgence and should not be factored in as the reason for Jihadists whose objective is to fight and Islamize Nigeria by introducing extreme form of sharia on 'infidels' should be granted amnesty. The irony is that all statements and commentaries by some of these leaders were received with mix- feelings (since some critics have expressed their disdain from this kind of statements that may not be appropriate as attacks by Boko Haram fighters are on the rise). Critics were pleased that the idea for amnesty has been dismissed while the campaign to rescue the kidnapped Chibok schoolgirls and end terrorism is on-going, and the focus of international community and the media.

CHAPTER 8

Opinions on Granting Amnesty to Boko Haram Members - Views from Eminent Politicians, Traditional & Religious Leaders.

Is amnesty for Boko Haram fighters that have killed more than 12, 000 innocent Nigerians and foreigners worth any consideration now or in the future? Does amnesty for Jihadists that their objective is to Islamize Nigeria change the deadly attacks by a terror group that Al-Qaeda even condemned their tactics of beheading of school boys and kidnaping schoolgirls? Should terrorists who have shed blood by killing innocent people be allowed to go free? What about the victims of Boko Haram's inhuman acts? What messages will be sent to the world about terrorists that are granted amnesty while individuals they killed and their families are not compensated or see justice take it due course. These questions were at a point being considered by Federal government of Nigeria even President Jonathan tells that world and believes that terrorists could not be negotiated with for no reason, other than it would empower them.

While Nigerians debated these questions, some Northern traditional, political, religious leaders were pressurizing President Jonathan to consider the option of granting terrorists amnesty and continue to witness the devastations therefore, Boko Haram is sustaining on the people and the nation. Some Nigerians, socially the opposition party to President Jonathan's Peoples Democratic Party (PDP), question the reasons for bringing the idea up (even as the negotiations were alleged to be going on privately). People questioned, is the debate on whether the group should be granted an amnesty a distraction by the Federal security agencies while the Joint Military Task Force set up by the president mobilizes to attack the terrorist? Would the amnesty get the military prepared for military offensive that may finally disrupt attacks by Boko Haram terrorists and stop it from spontaneous suicide bombings and open confrontations with security agents? While none of the answers to these questions was forthcoming, there were divided opinions whether granting amnesty or federal authority using all within its means to either apprehend or kill members of the group should resolve Boko Haram terrorism that has global networks. Majority of Nigerians favor military offensive to stop the Jihadists from sporadic attacks on innocent people by whatever means or tactics the federal authorities devised to achieve that goal. However, majority of the people against military action preferred dialogue first with the terrorists. The voices supporting dialogue and eventual amnesty for Boko Haram fighters were mainly from North.

The Sultan of Sokoto, Alhaji Muhammad Sa'ad Abubakar, the traditional leader of Sokoto Emirate and the religious head of Muslims in Nigeria was among the prominent Northern leaders calling for amnesty for the members of Boko Haram. The leader of Muslims in Nigeria made the call at a *Jama'tu Nasril Islam* (JNI) council meeting in Kaduna where he urged President Goodluck Jonathan to consider granting amnesty to the dreaded Islamic terrorist group. He disclosed that the amnesty would encourage the Jihadists to lay down their arms. In an apparent response to Sultan Sa'ad Abubakar's demand, President

Jonathan, in the epicenter of Boko Haram deadly operations, openly rejected the call for amnesty to the insurgents.

In a town-hall meeting in Damaturu, Yobe State, Jonathan was blunt to the Islamic and political leaders, government functionaries, and stakeholders, telling them: "you cannot declare amnesty to ghosts. Boko Haram still operates like ghosts. So you can't talk about amnesty for Boko Haram now until you see the people you are discussing with."[1] He explained that amnesty for the Niger Delta militants was possible because the militants came out of hiding to meet in person with late President Umaru Yar'Adua in Aso Rock (laying down their arms). However, not so for Boko Haram Islamic sect as no leader of the group has showed up for dialogue.

The Catholic Bishop of Sokoto, Most Reverend Matthew Hassan Kukah in his Easter message to his parishioners and Nigerians called for amnesty for the Boko Haram. Reverend Kukah who was a former Governor of Benue State in the Northern State of Nigeria, and also a former member of the Congress (House of Representative), remarked that "Many Christians have been tempted to use the persecution of Boko Haram, the destruction of Christian churches, and the brutal murders of fellow Nigerians as a justification for rejection of amnesty."[2] He disclosed, "Every true believer must understand that these sufferings, these trials are not outside the mind of God and His plans for our faith. The challenge is for us to remain faithful and steadfast so as not to be swayed by the dictates and exigencies of the moment."[3]

In an op ed. Easter message titled "Amnesty, Repentance, Forgiveness and Reconciliation," Rev Kukah also emphasized that persecution has been the hallmark of Christianity. International statistics data revealed that from the death of Christ more than 2000 years ago till date, some 70 million Christians have given their lives for Christ." "To reject amnesty is to place oneself at the same level as these miscreants. Their destruction on our country is not near the devastation of apartheid in South Africa. Yet, under President Mandela, Archbishop Tutu had to offer amnesty to leap frog the reconciliation process...The offer of amnesty will not solve all our problems, but it will bring us closer to a new dawn."[4]

Similarly, another respected clergy, the Catholic Bishop of Abuja, the capital city of Nigeria, Cardinal John Onaiyekan supported the call for amnesty. He remarked that it should be seen as a means of achieving peace in the North. He, however, said before the pardon should be considered, "members of the sect must seek repentance for the large number of person and property they have destroyed without any reason." Cardinal Onaiyekan in an Easter message noted that although the government had the power to give state pardon; it must be made with every caution. He remarked that Boko Hara fighters must seek forgiveness and repentance so that it would not look they did the right thing, and were persuaded to seek pardon from the state.

Cardinal Onaiyekan said, "as regards the case of an offer of amnesty to Boko Haram Jihadists, I understand that the security response in terms of arms, gadgets and trained personnel is helpful and necessary, but obviously not enough on its own. Government does well to reach out to all political forces and currents, so that the country can be on the same political page and jointly address this common menace, which terrorism is."[5]

Meanwhile, critics of these statements by Catholic leaders in support of prominent Northern leaders' call for amnesty for Boko terrorists were disappointed by these pleas when nobody was speaking for their victims. Opposition to the amnesty pleas was on the rise after statement credited to the Sultan. The Sultan who is the leader of the Jama'tu Nasril Islam (JNI) council – an Islamic religious organization that unites all Muslims in the country is a highly regarded individual whose words have relevance in all aspect of political and religious Islam. In essence, the weight of Sultan's statement is viewed as a consensus among Muslims in Nigeria. JNI is also regarded as the authority and forum through which policies that are political as well as religious emanate from Muslim leaders representing opinions of their followers in Nigeria.

Amidst the barrage of criticisms, majority of Nigerians decried the Sultan's request that President Goodluck Jonathan grant terrorist's amnesty, describing his plea for amnesty as unscrupulous. Chidi Eze, an Igbo from Southeastern Nigeria said that it is so unfortunate that Nigeria has become a place that anyone can kill, steal, and destroy and commit crimes against humanity and still get away with it. A leader of the pan-Yoruba socio-cultural group, Afenifere, Pa Reuben Fasonrati described the Sultan's call for amnesty as outrageous and highly unfortunate. He said, "I cannot imagine why a highly placed person in the caliber of Sultan should be seeking amnesty for Jihadists whose activities had rendered many people dead, others homeless and left thousands of children as orphans. "The sultan's call is obviously an indication that the caliphate is encouraging and condoning bloody violence…our position in Afenifere is that the Boko Haram members are evil. They should be identified and severely dealt with according to the laws of the land." [6]

Similarly, the Christian Association of Nigeria (CAN) rejected the proposal by the Sultan of Sokoto that members of the Boko Haram be offered amnesty. Speaking through its General Secretary, Dr. Musa Asake, CAN urged the Federal Government to rebuff the idea of any amnesty for the terror group. He wondered at the nature of amnesty the monarch was proposing for the terrorists. CAN, however, welcome the idea of Nigeria stakeholders to genuinely discuss the issues about Nigeria's development. It warned that for the talk about amnesty to hold water, the group must first renounce their extreme ideology and embrace the cease-fire plan. [7]

The Anglican Bishop of Wusasa Diocese, Bishop Buba Lamido, called for an overhaul of the CAN – the Christian body over its position on amnesty. In essence, he supported the granting of amnesty to Boko Haram fighters. His statement did not go well with CAN. The publicity secretary of the Christian Association of Nigeria (CAN) in the northern states, Elder Sunday Oibe responded to Bishop Lamido, and disclosed that there was no need for any amnesty for Boko Haram Jihadists who maimed and killed because they wanted to Islamize Nigeria.

While Bishop Lamido was reprimanding Christian Association of Nigeria (CAN) for insisting that President Jonathan grant amnesty to Boko Haram fighters, a newly installed Bishop of Akure Diocese Church of Nigeria, the Anglican Communion, Reverend Simeon Borokini, challenged the Jihadists to unmask themselves first before amnesty could be discussed. Borokini argued that as long as the group members are faceless, "it will be difficult for the Federal Government to grant amnesty to a faceless group." He, however, decried the level of insecurity brought about by terrorist attacks by group on Nigerians. The clergyman remarked that "The people should come out and show their faces as this would facilitate meaningful dialogue that anybody may want to have with them. "While regretting many lives lost as a result of attacks by Boko Haram terrorists, he asked the government to take a decisive action to stop the Jihadists from further killing of Nigerians.[8]

Bishop of Kubwa of Abuja Anglican Communion, Rt. Rev. Duke Akamisoko remarked that if the granting of amnesty would bring a lasting solution to the security challenges plaguing the north, it is worth consideration. "While we are looking at how to solve the problem, the terminology, amnesty, is what I'm not comfortable with. If the government wants to speak with them to know their grievances, fine!" He continued, "I do not agree amnesty should be granted because of the level of destruction of lives and property terrorists have inflicted on the people and the nation. What about the Christians who were slaughtered by the sect? What about the churches destroyed or set ablaze?"[9] Akamisoko asked?

The Northern Christian Elders Forum (NOSCEF) announced that the decision to grant amnesty to Boko Haram fighters "is a call to other radical groups in Nigeria to rise up in arms against their fatherland, to be blessed when such an act should be treated as treason." Chairman of the group, Evangelist Matthew Owojaiye argued that intimidating the Federal Government to grant amnesty is the highest display of hypocrisy and lack of patriotism. He remarked, "Are such people not indirectly admitting that they are the shadows or ghosts behind the Boko Haram? We totally object to even discussing amnesty when nothing has been done for the victims of the Boko Haram."[10]

Former Vice President of Nigeria Atiku Abubakar under President Olusegun Obasanjo's administration between 1999 and 2007 was asked in an interview whether he would, as a president grant amnesty to Boko Haram. He said that if he was the President, he would not hesitate to throw the ball into the court of the Boko Haram leaders. "

> As was case with the Niger Delta militants, I would declare amnesty for the sect members with a deadline within which to surrender their arms. With the expiration of the deadline, if the sect members don't lay down their arms, then my government would be in a better position to face its critics that accuse it of not taking the initiative." [11]

Atiku Abubakar, who is also a founding member of the ruling People's Democratic Party (PDP), the party which the president is also a leader remarked, "The deadline for the surrender of arms would show whether the Boko Haram fighters want peace or not."

President Goodluck Jonathan in his Easter message to Nigerians reiterated that members of the Boko Haram sect were not Muslims, According to him, there is no true adherents of Islam that would subject the country to killings, bombings, and other gory attacks the way Boko Haram had done. He remarked that from the terrorists' modus operandi, the sect members were products of international terrorism network and not members of Islam or any other religion in Nigeria.

> "Those who mindlessly and indiscriminately attack worship places, schools, health workers, motor-parks, banks and ordinary road users must be seen as they truly are: the brainwashed pawns of international terrorism." [12]

He emphasized that the terrorists do not represent any true religion or section of the country, and Nigerians must never play into their hands by succumbing to their nefarious ploys to incite religious, ethnic hatred and division among Christians and Muslims. He urged Nigerians to continue to exhibit restraint and understanding in the face of seeming provocations.

> "We must have peace, security and stability to effectively implement our agenda for national transformation in all parts of the country, and we shall continue to work ceaselessly to reestablish the prerequisite conditions for nationwide progress and development." [13]

He urged Nigerians to rededicate themselves to living in peace and oneness with all members of their communities, no matter their ethnicity, religious beliefs, or places of origin

Spokesperson of the US Bureau for African Affairs, Hilary Renner, disclosed the United States government is concerned about the on-going attacks against Nigeria's citizens, civil institutions, and infrastructure by Boko Haram insurgents. "The United States has already designated a number of Boko Haram's senior commanders as terrorists, shining a light on their horrific acts and cutting off their access to the US financial system.[14] She remarked that violent extremism requires more than just a security response. The group known as Boko Haram exploits legitimate northern grievances to attract recruits and public sympathy."[15]

Renowned American Civil Rights Activist, Rev. Jesse Jackson joined leaders that supported the Federal Government's decision to grant amnesty to Boko Haram fighters. On May 19, 2013, during an interview with journalists in Yenagoa, Nigeria, Jackson described the decision to negotiate amnesty with Boko Haram as a deliberate effort to end insecurity in the country. According to him, the amnesty offer must be open and honored, and implemented to include economic restitution. It must also include rebuilding churches and mosques and other structures destroyed by insurgents in Northern parts of the country. On the other hand, he remarked, within the United States, when there was civil unrest, there was a kind of state of emergency. "You can bargain and resolve the conflict in the North. You must have the ability to resolve conflict and not fight aggressively. It must not resolve into killing and being killed.[16]

The United States Secretary of State, Senator John Kerry also expressed concern about alleged human rights violations by Nigerian security forces fighting Boko Haram Jihadists. He raised the issue with President Goodluck Jonathan in an open discussion on May 25, 2013 when he sat beside President Jonathan at an African Union dinner in Ethiopia. His discussion on the security situation in Nigeria with President Jonathan publicly (in what international relations experts believed should have been a very private diplomatic dialogue) revealed the urgency and importance of the United States concerns. However, Senator Kerry defended Nigeria's right "to combat terrorism" but warned that Nigeria state security agents have to do so respect human rights." Prior to meeting with President Jonathan, Senator Kerry had also on May 17, 2013 took the unusual undiplomatic steps to publicly disclose that he "deeply concerned by credible allegations that Nigerian security forces are committing gross human rights violations, which, in turn, only escalate the violence and fuel extremism."[17]

Meanwhile, the former governor of Abia State, Orji Uzor Kalu joined in the amnesty debate for Boko Haram fighters. He renewed his calls for the amnesty. He disclosed that granting amnesty to the Jihadists is for the "best interest of Igbos." He remarked that when the

Niger-Delta militants emerged and were bombing pipelines and kidnapping people, the Federal government was able to sit down and negotiate with the group. He pointed out that because of the amnesty, the Niger-Delta area is peaceful and the source of Nigeria's oil money is protected from destruction. He disclosed that Nigeria cannot pay a price in one area (meaning amnesty to Niger-Delta militant) and not pay price in another (Boko Haram).

Former Governor Orji Kalu, who was raised and schooled in the Muslim North, remarked, "Let Boko Haram leaders come out like the Niger-Delta militants did, and the moment they do, should be granted amnesty. If you can give amnesty to the militants you can also give to Boko Haram."[18] He revealed that he would be willing to be a mediator and negotiate with Boko Haram if he was asked to do so for "the benefit of peace in Nigeria; for the benefit of my Igbo brothers who are being killed all over...You can see that if anything happens in any part of the world against Muslims, Igbo shops will be burnt in Nigeria. This is not fair. It is not justifiable." [19]

He also remarked that he is calling on northern elders, northern Ulamas, and all the people to come together and stop Boko Haram's criminal behaviour. He disclosed the Islam that he knows is not criminality; Islam preaches peace and unity. He cited examples of how relationships between Muslims and Christians, Hausa and Igbos had traditionally been.

> "During the civil war, my father had a lot of houses in the north, and when he came back after the war, some people who were looking after his houses; they counted all the monthly rents from the time he left and gave it to him. I am not holding forth for anybody but I am saying that is the quality of the good Muslim. So I believe that we should preach to our younger ones the values that we were known for."[20]

While the debate raged on whether the President Jonathan of Goodluck should grant amnesty to the terrorists, it was reported that on April 1, 2013 - Easter Sunday, the Jihadists ramped up their violent attacks in selected States in Northern Nigeria - particularly Kano, Bauchi and Borno State.   Sources pointed to the continued talk of amnesty by stakeholders within the federal government of Nigeria as the principle cause for the increased level of attacks because the Jihadists capture on the division among leaders in Nigeria along ethnic and religious lines to remain steadfast in the fight to Islamize Nigeria. Precisely, the division among leaders on how to fight and combat Boko Haram has continued to send wrong messages to the Jihadists.

Sources also revealed that the Jihadists have launched a broad mass recruitment campaign in the Kano State and its environs. The recruitment exercise was reportedly headquartered inside the ancient Islamic communities of Kano metropolis. The new recruits were taken to the troubled West African country of Mali for training. The training, it was gathered lasted between 4 and 6 months. A majority of the new recruits arrived Mali by road transport.

It was gathered that the leader of Boko Haram was recently a guest of a wealthy Islamic leader at a home located in the northern senatorial district of Bauchi State. The leader of the group had come to Bauchi to coordinate the Bauchi recruitment. They arrived in Bauchi two days before Easter Day on March 29 and according to security sources – departed to Mali on Easter Day. The recruitment exercise was reported to have netted the group more than 1,000 new members within 19 to 30 days of the recruitment exercise. Already the Jihadists have begun preparations for a Black June/July for the selected States in the Northern regions of Nigeria.[21]

With changing tactics and rising numbers of successful deadly attacks on the civilian population, police and military personnel casualties from ambush laid by Boko Haram fighters, the former Military Head of State of the Republic of Nigeria Major-Gen Muhammadu Buhari (rtd.), blamed insecurity in the country on the President Goodluck Jonathans administration. He Federal Government is poor handling of the economic and remarked that poor performance of the administration is the leading causes of political unrest in the country. General Buhari, who is also the leader of opposition party, Congress for Progressive Change told Hausa Radio Service of the British Broadcasting Corporation (BBC) in London that the problem of insecurity was not peculiar to the North alone, adding that there was no difference between the Boko Haram sect in the North and the militants in the South-South (referring to the Movement for the Emancipation of the Niger Delta (MEND) – the Niger Delta militants). According to him, "The world is very much concerned about two things - the problem of security and economic well-being of a nation. Security is number one. A country can only be economically viable if there is security. Nevertheless, how did all these crises start? How did the crises begin and assume this dimension?"[22]

He highlighted a connection between kidnapping and bombing. Buhari said that criminals abduct people and receive ransoms. He emphasized that "security is the responsibility of the state; they should know how these things came about."[23] Meanwhile, he urged President Goodluck Jonathan to persuade Boko Haram fighters to accept dialogue as a means of ending spiraling violence in the North. General

Buhari described the virulent sect, Boko Haram, as a creation of the present administration and urged the administration to stop blaming him (General Buhari) for the problem. He remarked that Boko Haram was a mark of failure of President Jonathan's administration.

In a response to the former head of State, the Minister of Information Mr. Labaran Maku said the amnesty being canvassed for Jihadists could only be considered when the group opens up for dialogue and negotiation. He maintained that amnesty could not be the first option when nobody from the sect has come out to discuss with the Federal Government. Mr. Maku explained that amnesty is usually an outcome of discussions and negotiations, whereby those being offered amnesty should accept the offer in principle with conditions attached. According to him, nowhere in the world has amnesty been offered unconditionally to a group that did not even come out to negotiate with the government. The Minister emphasized, "Amnesty could be part of the solution but can only come out of the process of dialogue and negotiations, but offering it unconditionally is not known."[24]

Maku warned that Nigerians should not over-politicize the issue. "People continue to compare it (Boko Haram) with the Movement for the Emancipation of the Niger Delta (MEND situation. We must not forget that amnesty for MEND came after a series of discussions and negotiations led by leaders of the Niger - Delta region and the combatants in the creeks."[25] He remarked it was after negotiations reached a certain point and there were commitments that the issue of amnesty was brought up. Amnesty, he remarked was not just offered without conditions and negotiation. Maku, therefore, urged politicians to see the issue of granting amnesty to Boko Haram as security and national issue. He warned that politicians seeking for votes in the on-coming election in 2015, and using such issues of national security not to unduly over-politicize this issue of amnesty.

As the debate whether Boko Haram should be granted amnesty seemed to be dividing the country especially with the powerful political and traditional leaders weighing in with their opinions, President Goodluck Jonathan summoned a Security Council meeting with his chiefs of the Armed Forces Council. After the meeting, the president eventually decided to appoint a committee to look into whether the group should be granted amnesty. The amnesty according to the office of the president, one of the primary conditions for consideration of an amnesty was that insurgents must come out and show their faces before any negotiation for an amnesty will take place.

Former head of state and national leader of the Congress for Progressive Change (CPC), Gen. Muhammadu Buhari, former heads of state,   Gen. Ibrahim Babangida, Gen. Abdulsalami Abubakar, the Sultan of Sokoto, Alhaji Sa'ad Abubakar, Catholic Bishop of Abuja, John Cardinal Onaiyekan and the leadership of the Northern Elders Forum (NEF) and other influential groups in the north (except the leadership of the Christian Association of Nigeria, CAN) welcomed the amnesty but the Jihadists rejected the offer.

Among North leaders who commended the president for setting up a committee to review the option to grant amnesty to Boko Haram was Hajia Turai Yar'adua, the widow of the former president of Nigeria, Umaru Musa Yar'adua. President Jonathan succeeded Yar'adua. Turai, urged President Goodluck Jonathan to forgive Jihadists as her late husband did to former militants in the Niger Delta. She remarked that when Yar'adua saw that the people in the Niger Delta, particularly the children were dying callously, he (Yar'Adua) took it upon himself to grant amnesty to the militants to ensure lasting peace.

> "There is poverty in the North. What Yar'Adua did in the Niger Delta, let Jonathan do the same thing to the North… Let him sit down and think about the insecurity in the North."[26]

Turai Yar'adua also advocated youth empowerment, emphasizing that if the youth are inspired, the country would be empowered as well. Meanwhile, President Goodluck Jonathan blamed leaders in the North (Muslims) for the continued Boko Haram violence. The President, made the remarks at an event that he was represented by the Minister of Special Duties and Inter-Governmental Affairs, Kabiru Turaki. He categorically remarked that leaders in the Northern States in Nigeria have not done enough to unmask those behind the group's activities.[27]

The Christian Association of Nigeria (CAN) criticized the President for his decision to set up a committee that will pave the way for amnesty for the Boko Haram Islamic sect. The Public Relations Officer of CAN (Northern states and Abuja), Mr. Sunny Oibe said,

> "If the government has decided to set up a committee to consider granting amnesty to Boko Haram under the watchful eyes of the National Security Adviser without compensating people that have been killed, it then shows that something is fundamentally wrong with our society and government.[28]

Mr. Oibe queried, how President Goodluck Jonathan said earlier he could not grant amnesty to ghosts not long ago, but all of a sudden decide to set up a committee for amnesty. He stressed during the time President Jonathan was the Vice President to Umar Musa Yar'Adua, their administration did not go about chasing the Niger Delta militants; rather the citizens from the South-South region went and talked to the militants to lay down their arms and engage the government constructively.

Oibe emphasized the question is: who are the members of this Boko Haram? He warned that if the issue of amnesty for Boko Haram was not handled with caution, the decision would encourage insurgencies throughout the country to rise and destabilize the country.

> "It means that if you have to get government's attention, you have to engage in lawlessness. The granting of amnesty to Boko Haram goes to show that lawlessness is a profitable venture in Nigeria. It will encourage the younger generation to embark on lawlessness so that government will give them attention.[29]

Mr. Oibe explained that as Christians from the North who have suffered from inhuman acts as a result of Boko Haram's insurgence, the president must be ready to engage the Christians because the silence of the church does not mean that Christians don't know what to do.[30] He remarked that Boko Haram members is not fighting because of poverty, unemployment and hunger, rather, they are killing people because they wanted to create an Islamic state where extreme forms of sharia are their laws.

President Jonathan inaugurated a 26-member "Presidential Committee on Dialogue & Peaceful Resolution of Security Challenges in the North." Their main task was to look into whether to grant Boko Haram amnesty and under what conditions. Dr. Reuben Abati, the Presidential Media spokesman said President Jonathan in inaugurating the committee has urged its members to constructively look into the possibilities of engaging key members of Boko Haram, and define a comprehensive and workable framework for resolving the crisis of insecurity in the country. Alhaji Taminu Turaki, the Minister for Special Duties was nominated as the chairperson. The committee's terms of reference included developing a framework for the granting of amnesty; setting up of a structure through which disarmament could take place and the development of a comprehensive victims' support programme and mechanisms to address the underlying causes of insurgencies that will help to prevent future occurrences."[32].

While the presidential committee was to sit for the first time, Boko Haram from its Maiduguri headquarters issued a statement rejecting any plans to meet with members of the committee. It disclosed that the Shura Council, the highest decision-making organ of the Jihadists led by Imam Abubakar Ibn Shekau is the only person who has the power to in their sect to decide whether Boko Haram fighters will accept the offer of amnesty. Boko Haram warned, "We rejected any form of amnesty stating that we did not ask for it. [33]

Another faction of the dreaded Islamic sect, Boko Haram, has rejected completely any proposed amnesty for the sect before the even the Federal Government made the offer. Abu Dardam, a spokesperson for Boko Haram faction told the BBC in an interview that the sect does not respect the Nigerian constitution and is only guided by the Qur'an. Dardam said the sect does not recognize democracy either as a form of government or as any institution operating under the system.34

Meanwhile, Borno State Commissioner of Home Affairs Information and Culture, Mr. Hyeladi Inuwa Bwala responded quickly and appealed to Boko Haram members to see reason and embrace the offer. However, security sources warned of the implications of granting amnesty to Boko Haram whose leaders have refused any representation and dialogue. Inuwa Bwala remarked, "Even if you look beyond the fragmented group of the terrorists, what happens if tomorrow, all the almajiris and jobless street urchins troop out in their millions and say they are *Boko Haram* and they want amnesty, which of course goes with a package of allowances, rehabilitation and training, could the government afford the cost? Does the government have the resources to cater to them? [35]

It is therefore the implications of negotiating amnesty as a tradeoff to terrorism that worries many Nigerians and the precedent that this may likely set presently and in the future in dealing with terrorists. However, as witnessed since the Presidential Committee on Dialogue and Peaceful Resolutions of Security Challenges in the North was inaugurated; there seemed to be no negotiations even though the committee was working modalities for the amnesty. Claims of negotiation with the Boko Haram was confusing as there were claims and counter claims of such meeting, but not established is what faction was at meeting to negotiate amnesty. However, it was gathered than an unknown faction was actually negotiating for amnesty with the federal government. What was not also clear was whether the group was negotiating under the group that is controlled by Shekua, the known leader of the main Boko Haram or someone else's personal or group gains.

Meanwhile, the offensive against Boko Haram by the Joint Military Task Force continued. Boko Haram has not given up its counter attacks. This is as evidence with the July 29, 2013 revealed. On this day, Boko Haram simultaneously attacked enclaves in Sabon Gari, Northern city of Kano state. Jihadists attacked the motor park with improvised bombing pipes. The area is known as the business and social spaces for convergence of Igbos and Christians from Southeastern Nigeria. Overall, the Igbos have been the most affected ethnic groups by Boko Haram attacks in terms of lives lost and property destroyed.

About 24 people were killed as a result of the attack. [36] On July 2014 in the same area of Sabon Gari was attack by suicide bomber that killed herself and 12 other people.

Overall, the Joint Military Task Force set up by President Jonathan was "gaining ground" in their offensive to dislodge Boko Haram. This was as news had it that Boko Haram splinter group has toppled Boko Haram's leader Abubakar Shekau. It was well-received news, but short-lived as the defiant Boko Haram leader emerged to announce that he was not dead. Shekau surfaced to make claims including the attacks in Abuja, Kaduna, and Lagos. He continued to show up regularly to broadcast his threats and determination not to release the kidnapped Chibok schoolgirls until the authorities set free his "soldiers," he claimed were captured and detained by the state security services.

When asked by reporters, whether the Presidential Committee on Dialogue and Peaceful Resolutions of Security Challenges in the North was justified since, the spiral of attacks by Boko Haram have not stopped rather increased, the chairman of the committee, Alhaji Taminu Turaki remarked," Is there a country in the world where the issue of terrorism has been resolved with the establishment of a committee….The issue of terrorism like the one in Nigeria, where we have many elements that are masquerading into it should not be resolved overnight. So it is something that has a lot of dimensions."[37]

For now, all the resources that the Federal government of Nigeria could gather, it has committed to dislodging Boko Haram. However, the Jihadists have successfully carried out multiple bomb blasts in Sabon Gari, where Igbos from Northeastern Nigeria reside, and have churches,   shopping   malls   and   entertainment   parlors destroyed. These are spaces where people converge in large numbers. Boko Haram also carried out violent attack in Kaka and Kakawa Local Government Areas of Borno less than 24 hours apart of these incidents.

On the same July 31, 2013, fisherman and traders were attacked and their property destroyed when insurgents attacked their villages. These orchestrated attacks in spite of the military offensive by the security forces have led to capturing majority of the Boko Haram fighters and forced majority of the villagers on the border town of Nigeria with Chad and Cameroon others to flee to neighboring African countries. The pursuit of Boko Haram fighters into the forest has not lowered the anxiety Nigerians have of their safety. People are still afraid and not guaranteed of their security in locations in the North and Central Nigeria and beyond - where Boko Haram has targeted.

The Sultan of Sokoto, Alhaji Sa'ad Abubakar condemned the attacks in Sabon Gari and Borno State. In a statement, he said that Jama'tu Nasril Islam (JNI) was baffled by the act of unleashing terror on human lives which continues unabated despite visible number of security check points mounted throughout the North and Central States in Nigeria. The Sultan who is the leader of umbrella organization holding together all Muslims in Nigerian said that the organization received with bewilderment, the news of the orchestrated multiple bomb blasts in Sabon Gari resulting in collateral damages and loss of lives. The Sultan described the attacks as reprehensible, inhuman and ungodly. He sent condolences to the families of the bereaved, the Government of Borno and Kano States, Shehu of Borno and the Emir of Kano.

In a statement, the Sultan who is also Muslim religious leader remarked, "We once again call on all concerned as a matter of urgency to nip in the bud future re-occurrences, which we don't pray for. As it is becoming more and more glaring to the right thinking person, there is a grand design to push the entire North into deeper crises and by extension of the Nigerian federation, the Emir warned"[38] He called for calm and restraint by citizens to avoid plunging the nation into tribal and religious confrontations. With the report of the Presidential Committee on Dialogue and Peaceful Resolution of Security Challenges in the North ready, but not officially available to the public, the Joint Military Force has shown no stopping in its campaign to dislodge Boko Haram, but at the same time, the precarious security situation witnessed in the country continues to rise.

While many Boko Haram's members have been captured or killed, there was no account of who is in charge of these splinter groups even when Boko Haram's leader, Abubakar Shekau was reported overthrown by a leader of another splinter group.   With Boko Haram's attacks still going on, following the same sporadic pattern of multiple bomb blasts - a symbol of Boko Haram Nigeria's - Al-Qaeda- style-operations, it is evident that the war on terror will not be won by military force alone. President Obama also reiterated during a town-hall meeting comments made in June 2013, while on a trip to South Africa. According to President Obama, the war on terror cannot be won by the use of military force alone. In essence, in a society where the people are deprived of their basic rights and needs and they are young and poor, the probability is high for persons facing these basic struggles to be persuaded by radicals to turn their back against the state. Rather than protect the sovereign state, they may likely be recruited, manipulated, and used to execute extremists' goals such as Boko Haram is espousing.

Therefore, the approach to resolving the problem of terrorism as international terrorism experts have warned is a holistic approach that is focused intelligence gathering and the use of force. The negotiation of amnesty for a terrorist group that has refused to show their faces or negotiate a truce is a wasted time and efforts, the experts revealed. Just as being poor or hungry does not make any person to rob a bank, the same as hunger should not or does not cause anybody to be a murder or a Jihadist. However, meeting the basic needs of the majority of the poor people may be one of the best motivations to stop Islamic radicalism. An unemployed youth that is looking for job to meet his basic needs of food, water, and shelter could easily be enticed by promises by clerics or fundamentalists that meet these needs. The teenager may likely be persuaded to adopt extreme values of his mentor. When government and citizens ensure that young people, who make up more than 65 percent of the population of Nigeria are given jobs, the probability that the attraction to radicalism or crime would be drastically reduced.

In Northern Nigeria where the problem of unemployment is more pronounced and often by culture, people are prone to loyalty to elders or clerics – even without the largesse of providing these basic needs, any little incentive may probably win huge loyalty. When the teenagers are motivated with cash and other religious and material incentives such as free Islamic education, travels and cash offers in grants and scholarships, the indoctrination process becomes much easier to accomplish when the objective for these gifts is wrapped with religion.

When unemployed teenagers are lured with incentives and brainwashed, they believe that committing suicide bombing with rewards in paradise was the ultimate decisions for them. When the individual kills self to achieve the jihadists' goal of Islamization and getting rid of 'infidels,' he goes to paradise; this kind of indoctrination using religion to achieve the selfish goals of the Jihadists is not just very dangerous, but a serious threat to national security of Nigeria, the United States, The United Kingdom or elsewhere that terrorism is promoted.

Therefore, reducing the threats posed by Jihadists [like Boko Haram] needs a holistic approach from political, cultural, economic, social and ethnic perspectives. Since issues revolving around these factors could be used to create problems that would threaten the sovereignty of a nation, mixing these problems and adding religious and ideological beliefs makes the matter a double tragedy for a nation. When these problems extremists exploit to motivate wannabe terrorists are not addressed by governments, political and religious leaders and other stakeholders including businesses and entrepreneurs giving jobs to young people, the likelihood that terror will be eliminated in Nigeria or elsewhere is not likely to happen. Today, it may be al-Qaeda type-terrorists; tomorrow, it may be either a mutated form of Islamic fundamentalists or Christian-conservative evangelists engaging in its form of crusade to establish bases in Nigeria or elsewhere. The world has witnessed these acts of violence in history; Boko Haram may not be the last of these fundamentalists groups as long as we allow the problems we should have taken care, and individuals that exploit them, including   Nigeria youth's vulnerability to fester for that long.

CHAPTER 9

Nigeria – Shading the Image of a Failed State

Some of the root causes of the religious and sectarian violence in Nigeria may after all not have anything to do with religion, rather all to do Nigeria Constitution and the unresolved problems from the manner more than 250 tribes were forced to live together without plans to address difficulties emanating from the relationships. Therefore, understanding some of the real causes of so-called religious and political tensions in the country is an important step to finding solutions to these inherent problems destabilizes Nigeria. If these problems remain unresolved, pundits worry that the fragmentation of the country as a failed state as predicted is imminent.

However, others disagree - informing that Nigeria has overcome some of her most difficult political and religious problems, and survived them. Many others doubt whether the present violence in the name of terrorism by individuals or groups will predict better future for the country. General Don Idada Ikponwen is the former Provost Marshal of the Nigerian Army and is considered as one of the country's leaders. In an interview with Nigeria leading Newspaper, the *Vanguard* he remarked,

> "Let me say pointedly that it is no longer an issue for argument whether Nigeria has turned a terrorist state or not. Nigerian government does not promote terrorism as a policy, but Nigeria has become a terrorist enclave, where terrorists operate either on their own or in conjunction with terrorists outside the region."[1]

General Ikponwen, an attorney and a security expert disclosed that Nigeria has become a terrorist state and as a result, citizens are losing their lives. "We are losing unquantifiable lives and properties, we are losing self-esteem, we are losing our past glory to this perilous state of thriving terrorism in Nigeria."[2] He suggested for Nigeria to move forward, it must address the state of insecurity in the country. He explained that government and leadership at all levels must be seen as making concerted effort to create an environment where crime and terrorism will be unattractive.

General Ikponwen said, "Terrorism whether they are from the North or the East is terrorism. It is the use of violence to attempt to overwhelm the legitimate government to prove that a legitimate government is bad and inefficient to win the heart of the people. Terrorism is based on deep-rooted anger and disaffection."[3] He remarked that the primary purpose of government is to provide security and guarantee the welfare of the people. According to him, when government is perceived to be incapable of providing the security and guaranteeing the welfare of the people, the inevitable conclusion is that government is ineffective. He said, "Let me put it more succinctly; there is no government unless that government is efficient."

According to General Ikponwen the events happening in Nigeria, "the killings, robbery, murder, assassinations, kidnappings that flood the land, many of which the culprits are not traced or brought to book; with the way that stealing has become the order of the day, especially among highly placed individuals in government, when these people are not brought to book, when nothing serious is being done even to act as deterrence." He continued, " the way that people are amassing wealth and nobody is asking questions; the way that materialism has become the essence of life; the way that there is much vacuum in the system." Furthermore, he remarked, "the way that people find solutions to problems and nobody takes them seriously; the way that we create establishments and bring unserious people to run them; the way that we make government look as if it is there to serve the interest of those who are always friends of government, people who Nigerians call friends of any government in power; we as a nation have become a laughing stock, not only among Africans but the world at large. I believe that we cannot continue this way. The morale of well-meaning Nigerians is at its lowest."

World Christian and Muslim Leaders task Nigerians to Peaceful Co-exist

After days of deliberations by scholars from within and outside Nigeria on the situation in the country and what could be done to restore peace and order following Boko Haram repeated attacks and massacre of innocent people, the World Muslim League (WML) made a public statement. The group advised Nigerians to rekindle the once mutual understanding that existed among Nigerians irrespective of their religion, creed, and region.

The Boko Haram's violence also got the attention of the Vatican on Easter Sunday, May 31 2013. The new Catholic pontiff, Pope Francis in his Easter message - prayed for Nigeria. In his remarks, he said, "Let us remember in our prayers, those where great numbers of people, including children, are held hostage by terrorists groups"[4] This was an apparent reference to a French family kidnapped in Cameroon and believed held hostage in April 2013 by Boko Haram. The Pope called for peace among people of diverse religions and tribes. Among the hostages held at that period by Boko Haram was a French family of seven people, including the family head, Tanguy Moulin-Fournier. They were tourists and had visited a park in Northern Cameroon when they were abducted and brought to Nigeria by Boko Haram militants.[5] The hostages were later released. It was gathered the French government paid a ransom that the United States and some other Western countries have opposed the ransom as United State saw exchange of money for kidnaped Westerners as encouraging more terrorism that may be attracted by these incentives.

An Islamic group, Muslim Rights Concern (MURIC), supported amnesty for the dreaded Islamic sect, Boko Haram. The director of the group, Prof. Ishaq Akintola, said that amnesty was a viable solution to the sect's insurgency and terrorism. He remarked that such an initiative was needed to shield Nigeria from a second civil war, and possibly, a military coup. MURIC justified its support for amnesty because, according to the statement, it stands for peace, and gives life, hope and recovery.

On the continued hostility by insurgents, with rising daily death toll and insecurity all over North and Central states in Nigeria, MURIC said. "Terrorists have one mindset, namely, to put asunder what government has put together, to destroy what government has built," it remarked. "Terrorists seek to create much havoc as possible in order to attract attention to their causes," MURIC concluded. The group reminded the anti-amnesty camp that there is a serious implication of a total rejection of amnesty. "This includes the possibility of escalation of violent attacks which may culminate in a second civil war with its dire consequences,"[6] it warned.

Boko Haram Terrorists – Impact on Relationships Among Tribes in Nigeria

Governor Rotimi Chibuike Amaechi of Rivers State is among few state governors in Nigeria with records of achievement. Despite his accomplishments, and being cast in doubt by opposition party in the muggy waters of politics in Nigeria, he remains one of the "action" governors and a credible leader in the country where these accolades are hard to come. In an interview, he remarked Nigerians have no guts for revolution. "Yes, revolution can happen outside Nigeria. However, here, I do not think so." He stressed, "Tell me what happened in Sudan, Libya, Zimbabwe, and other countries that have not happened here. Our elasticity has no limit. You do not pray for electricity to be regular but you know that some Nigerians pray 'God, let the light be stable today.' We pray without working to solve our problems and we think God will do what we are supposed to do for us."[7]

These statements were made at an event organized in Western part of Nigeria. Governor Amaechi is from Rivers State in the South-South Nigeria. Three days earlier before governor Amaechi's comments were made, a militant group, the Movement for the Emancipation of the Niger Delta (MEND) based in Nigeria South killed 12 Policemen in Bayelsa the home state of the president Jonathan of Nigeria. Initially, there was no claim of responsibility for the crime, however, on April 8, 2013; MEND claimed its members carried out the attack on the police officers. Critics believed that the debate over amnesty for Boko Haram Jihadist might have motivated this particular attack. It was not immediately known the origin or tribes of the police officers killed, but many believed that MEND was equally seeking attention granted to Boko Haram during the debate and counter arguments about whether Boko Haram fighters should be granted amnesty or not.

CNK news editorial commentary asked, "Bravery" in killing our Policemen....would the president be granting Niger Delta Militants amnesty just as he planned to grant Boko Haram?" From the comments, it may seem that there is no end to the violence in Nigeria, but the experiences from Nigeria's history showed that Nigeria like Governor Chibuike Amaechi, who is also perceived as an agent of social change is addressing what is truly Nigeria's character.

Multi-Religion, Multi- Problems – Boko Haram' s Exploitation of Nigeria' s Diversity

The United States is a very good example of a homogeneous society. Yes, homogeneity is a critical factor that sustains nations and even marriage between two individuals. When one talks of homogeneity, it should not be isolated to race or ethnicity alone. The so-called ethnic nationalities in America are too thin that the general American dream assimilates them. When you talk of homogeneity, you think of language, literacy, religion, directive principles, and values and of course ethnicity.

In the United States over 90% speak and understand English, about the same figure can transform their thoughts in writing, and an overwhelming majority are Christians. This is homogeneity because birds of the same feather flock together. Nigeria is a nation with 50% Muslim and 50% Christians. The diversity could be exploited or harnessed for reasons that may develop the country or destroy the sovereignty of the nation. In the case of Boko Haram, the use of the same religion to divide people is what the terror group exploits when it targets Christians and their worshipping place to execute suicide bombings on the holiest of the seasons such as Easter Sunday and Christmas eve-bombing of Churches when the spaces are full of worshippers. The same as the attack of Motor Parks, residential and entertainment spaces areas where the Igbos reside or converge in large numbers. The suicide bombings at Sabon Gari bombing, and the attacks on passenger cars carrying Igbos traveling from North to Eastern Nigeria are signifiers of targeted `assaults.

CHAPTER 10

Terrorism & Sectarian Violence - A Reflection on Nigeria`s Past, Present & Ways Forward

---

A critical look at Nigeria history reveals that the amalgamation of South and Northern protectorates – Christians and Muslims has led to ethnic and religious conflicts which groups such as Boko Haram capitalizes to propagate their ideology, and gain support in their jihad to Islamize Nigeria. Like the rise of fundamentalism in the North, Jihadists have use religion as undercover to express tribalism that shaped Nigeria's history including the leading causes of sectarian violence.

The origin of some of the events in Nigeria's history is attributed to relationships between the North and South on political and religious lines, the relationships of leaders and people within these frames. Moreover, how the Nigeria constitution interpreted these relationship. On another note, the relationship of the South (Christians) with the West by culture and religion - pre and post-colonial experiences is also part of the problem. However, the most identified and unresolved problems causing most of the sectarian and political problems in Nigerian remains the amalgamation of tribes and regions by the British without negotiated arrangement between people that were being joined together.

Other problems destabilizing Nigeria included years of military dictatorship and its domination of power that some perceived was clueless to finding solutions to economic problems facing the country. With poor leadership of the ruling political class, and the masses [that were hopelessly intimidated and frustrated by directionless regimes], the neglect of the economy and in fractural growth were accumulated problems that contributed to building tensions that the present democratic administration inherited. The unfortunate development is Nigerians wanted quicker answers and solutions to their problems that took long time to accumulate. With people demanding quicker results, analysts identified lack of patience on the part of citizens as the frustration building up to undermine the little or major positive things government is doing to correct the mistakes of the past. However, critics disagreed, emphasizing the revenue Nigeria derives from oil export every month is enough to overcome Nigeria's problems or reduce them to the minimum.

Economists agree that average person on the street should feel the impact of government – if not directly on their lives with the wealth, she derives from export of petroleum products and gas. Nigerians they emphasized should have access to loans or capital apart from meeting their basic needs. Government, they emphasized must provide the foundation to make these things happen. It is this state of hopelessness that pushes people to seek leadership change, and election of politicians into office that ushers in economic prosperity.

The track of Nigeria's history reveals a porous national foundation with underlying unresolved ethnic and religious problems. These problems continue to affect peace, stability, and economic development of a nation with abundant human and natural resources to be one of the greatest economies of the world. Nigeria has the potentials of becoming the world economic power, but it will not be realized until the economic growth reflects on lifestyle of the people.

On religious fundamentalism and impact on Nigeria's economic development, there is no doubt that the impact of terrorism could be enormous even as the violence is concentrated in North and North Central States in Nigeria. While economic activities in the South are active, there are goods and services that come from North that help to maintain Nigeria's economy. The disruption of flow of good and services by Boko Haram terrorists is affecting Nigeria's economy. With the terrorists often capturing the photo opportunities on the media, the Jihadists are scaring away foreign investors. The media by making the voices of terrorists heard sends messages that disseminate their agenda of theocracy and fear that the Jihadists wanted to spread. The aftermath of these extremists' imposition of their views and agenda on the people is that they have no regard or respect for the opinions of a majority that hold different views from their extreme interpretation of sharia including moderate Muslims. They give no clue, cared less how their terror affects people's lives, investments and Nigeria's economy.

Leaders in Nigeria seem not to help to diffuse the extremists' religious views that violence arising from Jihadists does not just start overnight. No Nigerian leader, past and present will feign ignorance that he is not away that religious fundamentalism breeds in North and South Nigeria, with the Muslim extremists being the most violent. However, the same leaders that are aware of these deadly extremists in the North want to turn their attention elsewhere thinking that the problem posed by fundamentalists will go away. Some of them wanted to be politically correct by not interfering with religion until violence (as witnessed with Boo Haram) manifests on the streets and it becomes too late to prescribe a panacea that would have resolved the problem from the beginning when the extremists had little resources, power and influence.

Regrettably, in Nigeria religion and politics are always inseparable manifestations. When leaders play politics with religion, it brings about intolerance; diversity in communication among the people is relegated to the back burner. When tolerance and diversity are not discussed as a key national development program, the lack of awareness that diversity communication is a huge sector that needs investment of time and money is part of Nigeria's problem. The result of lack of diversity programs is that divergent views and opinions are not tolerated. The dialogue that respects for others views or a little sensitive would have maintained the discussion often fails. The frustration, the anger from all sides not voicing their opinions escalate already tensed situation, thus the violence on streets witnessed on the streets including the violence after the cancellation of Miss World pageant in Nigeria in 2002. The fundamentalists hijacking of the rhetoric led to rioting and killing of 200 Nigerians. The pageant was eventually cancelled and moved to Britain. The fact that Nigeria is yet to come to terms with her past – psychological trauma of colonization by the British has seemingly left red eyes on Nigeria.

Nigerians history still affects events that spin the nation into controversies and often lead to escalation of violence, the loss of lives and property. When the subject is about religion, politics, the recall of past relationships among tribes brings in hostility to people who resort to violence, thus threatening the security of the nation.

The mistrust among citizens also raises conspiracy theories, suspicion and controversies. These conspiracy theories, suspicions and controversies have defined and affected Nigerians and how they relate to one another. The rise of Boko Haram and other fundamentalist groups in Nigeria have deep roots to Nigeria's history of religious extremists and their agenda of creating Islamic state or caliphate. As witnessed with Jihadists in Afghanistan, Iraq and now Syria, these groups metamorphose and as new ones form, the more deadly and technologically sophisticated they are. It is the reason why international community should not be treated in isolation what is happening in Nigeria with what is currently going on with Jihadists around the world.

With Nigeria and the fight against Jihadists, the past should be considered in shaping the future. Bok Haram in mounting their flag in a town in Maiduguri it captured and fully in control on August 23, 2014 is like ISIS in Iraq and Syria declaring their caliphate state. How the world reacts to these developments, will prediction the future – whether the global village is going back to 400 years history when Jihadist conquered and captured towns and cities in Middle East and Africa – and was heading to Europe but ended up in Turkey.

The loss of one of the opportunities to host Miss World pageant was in 2002. Due to fundamentalist's rioting 200 lives were lost and forced the event to be moved to London. The experience cannot be treated in isolation of Boko Haram's agenda of Islamization of Nigeria by introducing extreme forms of sharia in Nigeria. Bok Haram was founded in 2002. The birth of the terror group in 2002 and the rioting that saw the "parading of naked women" as against the Islamic sharia cannot be separated from the ideology that Western influence is sinful– which in Hausa language is what Boko Haram means. The coincidence touches on various historical facts to illuminate the circumstances surrounding Nigeria's short sightedness about the fundamentalists' agenda and how these radicals have played authorities. For authorities not to be aware of these brewing problems until they unleash terror is self-denial. The key question remains, why events that set Nigeria backward to Stone Age still repeat? These events have not only shaken Nigeria's history but tested the zeal of her people and the nation's interpretation of order, peace, unity and gravity as a stable nation.

Whatever lessons (if any) that Nigerians may learn from Boko Haram threats will shape her future. How Nigeria handles the Jihadists will influence Nigeria's history, and shape her future. Reflections about the past showed Nigeria has not experienced terrorism of any magnitude as Boko Haram. However, she can learn from the playbook on Iraq and Afghanistan to deal with the threats posed by Boko Haram. Since Nigeria is limited to how far it could wage the war against Boko Haram, the presence of the international community to assist provide logistics, intelligence and military assistance to rescue the Chibok kidnapped school girls is a welcome development.

As earlier postulated, the presence of the international experts on the campaign mission to rescue the Chibok schoolgirls should extend to fighting war on terror. This is as long as countries involved stay clear of the internal politics in Nigeria. Their role is crucial to the success of war against Boko Haram and terrorist in the West Africa region. Nigeria's stability is important to global political and economic stability. How Nigeria handles Boko Haram and try to correct its past mistakes will reveal her determination to be a regional power, but also a power to be reckoned with in global politics. Nigeria economy and innovative strengths on the rise may be limited by circumstances, how she deals with its past and its internal and external threats. Finding ways forward is only a decision Nigerians and their leaders must have to make.

Nigeria: Which Way Forward?

Nigeria could move forward if it protects herself from both internal and external threats that affect every aspect of her economy and lives of the people. On August 7, 1998, two massive bombs exploded outside of the U.S. embassies in Dar es Salaam, Tanzania, and Nairobi, Kenya, nothing was known about the terrorist group operating in Nigeria; thus, responsibility for the attacks was quickly attributed to Al-Qaeda.

Less than four years later, Al-Qaeda operatives struck again, killing 15 in an Israeli-owned hotel near Mombasa, Kenya, simultaneously firing missiles at an Israeli passenger jet taking off from Mombasa's airport. The United States was startled by the attack, thus, the response to send a message that such assaults will not go unpunished. It was based in the conviction to take the fight to the terrorists' bases in Afghanistan and Iraq that ultimately led to the "War on Terror." On Nigeria's part, the country is yet to develop high-level intelligence surveillance system to monitor its enemies coming from across her borders in Africa and overseas to cause trouble in the name of Jihadists' movement or Muslim brotherhood.

After the September 11, 2001 destruction of the World Trade Center, it became obvious that Al-Qaeda's handwriting was on the walls of attack that brought down the World Trade Center. The United

States decided to take the War on Terrorism beyond U.S. borders to Iraq and Afghanistan. According to former U.S. Ambassador to Nigeria, Princeton Lyman, in a peer-reviewed article authored with J. Morrison on *Foreign Affairs* journal remarked that the Bush administration has designated the greater Horn of Africa a front-line region in its global war against terrorism and has worked on dismantling Al-Qaeda infrastructure there.   Lyman and Morrison explained the war on terror was going on, that the U.S. failed to recognize less visible terrorist threats in Africa:

> "Countering the rise of grass-roots extremism has been a central part of U.S. strategy in the Middle East, but the same has not generally been true for Africa"[1]

The authors also disclosed that Nigeria's Islamic challenge comes from a combination of religious, political, and economic factors. He remarked that Northern Nigeria with the Hausa-Fulani is primarily Muslim and has influential Muslim brotherhoods in Western Africa region and the Middle East. According to Lyman, after Nigeria's independence in 1960, Northerners dominated the political and military establishment. Throughout this period, however, the authors explained that Nigeria has retained a delicate balance between Muslims, and the mostly Christian population from the South. That balance is profoundly tested in the 21st century as a more fundamentalist brand of Islam asserts itself in key areas of the country.

> "This resurgence is partly the outcome of an internal
>   debate which begun in the 1960 and fueled by religious
>   scholars funded by Saudi Arabia – over the purity of
>   Nigerian Islam. But an equally important factor is the
>   changed political and economic fortunes of the north." [2]

With Nigeria's position in global affairs, the 2002 religious rioting that began when fundamentalists opposed to the idea of hosting of Miss World pageant, coincided with the time the U.S., under George W. Bush administration designated the Horn of Africa as a front-line region in his global war on terrorism. President Bush has worked to dismantle Al-Qaeda infrastructure in the continent. However, since the U.S. failed to recognize the presence of other less visible terrorists' threats in the continent, the existence of these less visible terror groups in Nigeria were responsible for the Miss World 2002 rioting that killed more than 200 Nigerians. That invisible terrorist group has since metamorphosed into Boko Haram and its splinter group such as *Jama'atu Ansarul Musilimina Fi Biladis Sudan* or "Vanguards for the Protection of Muslims in Black Africa".

Lyman and Morrison theses indicated that Nigeria intelligence should have been award of threats posed by Boko Haram for a very long time. In essence, for Nigeria leadership to feign ignorance on the root causes of terrorism in Nigeria is doubtful and unreasonable. Nigeria's leaders should also be aware that Nigeria is an emerging democracy that is gradually becoming regional and continental power. The authors warned Nigeria leaders to recognize that the country's stability requires addressing the unprecedented levels of poverty, and underdevelopment in the country – the major causes of conflict in the country.

While the Horn of Africa was designated as fragile nation where terrorists unleashed their terror; Nigeria leaders must be proactive with their strategies to arrest terrorists' assaults that project the image of a nation that has joined the league of unstable nations threatened by insurgents. They include Sudan, Eritrea, Ethiopia, Somalis,

Djibouti, Uganda, Tanzania, and Kenya.[3] Nigeria may be richer than most of these countries, but to eliminate terrorist threats not just in the Horn of Africa, but also in Nigeria. The United States. and European nations such as Germany, France, and the U.K. must join hands to address the continent's economic and political problems, not just with sending tactical and intelligence team to rescue the kidnapped Chibok schoolgirls in Nigeria. Reducing trade barriers and allowing more goods from Africa is one sure beginning to addressing problems in the continent. Direct investments by Western countries in some of the stable African nation are still very low.

As Ugandan President, Yoweri Museveni said during a White House visit on June 10, 2003, Africa does not need aid; they need the economic doors of the U.S. and Europe to unlock to African goods.[4] He emphasized "subsidies," cheap pricing of goods and services produced by farmers from the continent are few of the undermining factors that stifle Africa's economic development. He went further to show Africans work very hard, especially farmers, but due to underpricing, their products do not generate any income. In other words, his remarks were that Africa toils for Europe and the U.S.

As nature has a way of balancing acts, Museveni's statement should not be taken at face value because what goes around may come around, sometimes haunt us more over a long period time. The West and China may be benefiting from cheap labor and pricing of African products but along the way, we may pay heavy price for the poverty we created by neglect or isolating Africa. With such reasoning, we need to act now before it is too late. Africa must be recognized as part of the international community, leaders need proactive actions to market their countries' goods and services on the international market in exchange for hard currency that will provide revenues for other services including rehabilitation of manufacturing sector, infrastructure development, jobs and security.

Foreign aids and handouts do not sustain any economy in a short or long term. Trade, economic growth, and investments do. Presidential visits by U.S. and European leaders to Africa either are not enough. While it may give the president's views of Africa's problems, action is what matters and required most to see cash from in to the continent from other revenue –earning sources other than exports of minerals and natural resources. Africa must also not be treated in isolation as a destitute or a panhandler for foreign or international assistance to fight diseases and famine. She actually has resources from petroleum, gold, diamond, and precious stones, just to name a few, so she has many commodities to trade with the rest of the world.

Many African countries rank high among world producers of cash crops such as cocoa, coffee, and tea. As Museveni pointed out, poor pricing has denied Africa from benefiting financially from exports. Therefore, the impression that Africa must be granted aid (financial assistance) is ridiculous and must be dropped. Because, when media attention focuses on wars, diseases and disasters, the eyeballs of the world through media attention shifts attention from root causes of major African problems. On the raging wars that often frame Africa's image, the big question is who supplies these wars lords with arms when barely they have no money to feed few years (before they picked arms to fight), and suddenly they are in wealth and caring for large contingents of once, hungry, rag-tagged youth that suddenly turned into 'militias' or killing machines.

Listening to some of the media-talk shows and news commentators on the heights of the campaign on war on terror, orders were issued with video clips showing the military intercepting ships on the high seas of the Mediterranean and Pacific Ocean. This search for arms caches going to Al-Qaeda or other organizations designated by the U.S. State Department as terrorist groups is no doubt helpful in the campaign to ensure that weapons do not get into the hands of terrorists.

Regrettably for decades violence (military coup d'état, armed-uprisings, tribal warfare) reigned in parts of Africa -   African warlords, previously addressed by some Western nations as "freedom fighters" have imported arms from Europe, Russia, China, and the U.S. without problems. Most weapons end up not necessarily in the hands of organized armies, but in the hands of child soldiers and fundamentalists. Even at the end of guerilla warfare (in some cases after civil war and after toppling of dictators such as in Libya), these arms remain unaccounted. Most of the weapons eventually find their way into the hands of bandits, allowing a repetitive circle of violence; taking more casualties than before.

The world may be witnessing the dismantling of terrorist networks, but with millions of arms floating in the open and black markets, not just in Africa, but in unsafe parts of the world, they provide easy instruments for terrorists and bandits to carry out, robbery, kidnapping, assaults, assassinations, street gang fights and wars. This violence affects not just Africans but people of different nationalities, their national interests, and the global community. When we live in an unprotected neighborhood, it affects directly or indirectly the value of our property and our quality of life in general.

Nigeria Joint Military Task Force against Boko Haram military raided a house in Barunde of Gombe in Northern Nigeria supposedly belonging to a member of Boko Haram on April 5, 2012. The security operatives seized 51 rocket launchers in a house used to manufacture rockets and improvised explosive devices (IEDs).[5] With these violence as witnessed in parts of Africa, there is no way any nation impacted by violence would sustain economic growth now and in the future.

Should security of Africa be left to Africans alone? While Africa accounts for 6 of the 10 countries with the fastest economies of the 21st century, these countries witnessing economic prosperity are changing the scope of their economic development; peace and stability remain the most important elements among others that have seen these countries develop. In essence, African nations require stability that brings about development. However, Africa still faces more challenges with the menace of terrorists than it has in its history. It is not just with Boko Haram in Nigeria, but fundamentalists across the continent in countries such as Eritrea, Ethiopia, Mali, Egypt, Libya, Tunisia, Algeria, Somalia, Djibouti, Uganda, Tanzania and Kenya.

With the connection of these Jihadists to their counterparts in Middle East and the oil money now available to the Jihadist groups in Iraq and Syria, there is need for a joint force of the African continent to reduce the menace of terrorists, now that some of them are becoming more dangerous than Al-Qaeda in Iraq and Afghanistan. The presence of international technical, security experts in Nigeria to rescue the Chibok missing schoolgirls is a positive development; however, fighting terrorism needs a complete focus, huge financial support and consistent timeless pursuit. In essence, fighting Boko Haram or any terrorists in Nigeria or Africa must be a sustained commitment by international community in support of countries experiencing this violence. It is important to also explain that the countries threatened by Jihadists must provide the leadership with international support.

Côte d'Ivoire fell into a political quagmire that destroyed all that former President Félix Houphouet-Boigny created for a country that used to be the model of Africa's democracy. Beautifully planned and maintained, it earned the nickname, the "Paris of Africa." It was a true example of what African countries ought to be politically. However, Cote d' Ivoire is yet to recover from war resulting from a presidential election mess that almost split the country into North and South, it was an example of an African nation that witnessed economic development through its own trade in its endowed natural resources.

The world witnessed how the exploitation of tribal sentiments and the dichotomy almost led to Cote d'Ivoire almost becoming a failed state. Nigeria must learn from lessons of countries around the world that conflict and Jihadists have devastated that they may not recover any time soon or ever. Nigerians must therefore not allow their country be destroyed by forces that have nothing at stake or have interest of the country, rather have clandestinely worked toward their agenda of disintegrating the country.

In Europe and elsewhere around the world, nations are merging and combining resources as buffers to unstable domestic and global economies. At a time when nations are clamoring to create larger economic and political unions for strength and stability, Nigeria cannot afford to break apart. Years ago, it was unthinkable that Eastern bloc countries would ever join the European Union; today, it is a fact despite economic setbacks and financial meltdowns. However, merging nations do not just provide security but also economic advantages and global connections that are required for nations to stay alive in depreciating wealth around the world. Africa must embrace these economic and political realities of the 21st century in terms of economic and political collaborations and sharing common currencies.

In the absence of economic wealth, equitable distribution of wealth, poverty prevails; hence, Africa becomes fertile ground for recruitment by fundamentalists and extremists. In Africa, with more than 4,000 tribes, each group with its differences and idiosyncrasies, the expectation that desperation and tension caused by poverty would not lead to rioting, tribal/community clashes, killing and maiming would be foolhardy. In essence, it would be imaginable that peace will always prevail under these deplorable conditions. There is no doubt some use religion as a shield to steer hate and anger against their neighbors, others use the gun to start conflicts we witness around the world. Politicians want to win elections at all costs, including using character, verbal and physical assassination of opponents to have advantage over opponents.

In Africa, where guns and ammunitions are easily available from all over the world at 'buy-one-get-one-free prices,' the attraction of prospective insurgents, terrorists and war lords is overwhelming, leading to these individual exploring war as viable option to achieve their selfish goals and exploiting the vulnerable – the youth of their country to achieving their selfish goals. Similarly, the more failed states in Africa, the more easy access to spaces (countries) for terrorists ejected from Middle East and African troubled states such as

Egypt, Somalia, Libya, Mali, are ready to invade and occupy new vulnerable countries. There are also some African countries not on the list of vulnerable or failed States, yet the fundamentalist clerics have made so much in roads into them with their spread of extreme forms of their religion. Some of the youths have been brain-watched by these clerics; others have been won over by promises of jobs and financial security to the unemployed among their recruits.

In some parts of Africa, even where the government seems to be in charge of the sovereignty of the state, poor people (mainly youth) neglected by their governments have sought the mullahs and fundamentalists clerics as their only hope. This last group of recruits by fundamentalist makes the work of recruits by Jihadists much easier. The fear and what should be of concern to the global community is that some of the Jihadists' recruits are no longer children or youth from economic under-privileged class. The aborted attacks on board Northwest Airline's Flight 253, en route from Amsterdam to Detroit and the arrest of Umar Abdul Mutallab referred as the "Underwear-Bomber," highlighted the growing radicalization of children of rich people, not really born in Nigeria but with a Nigerian background.

The suspected terrorist in the Northwest Airline's flight helps to unravel the fears that experts on terrorism have expressed about the growing apostles of Osama Bin Ladin and their dispersion across the globe. Al-Qaeda in the Arabian Peninsula (AQAP) claimed to have organized the attack with Abdul Mutallab; they said they supplied him with a bomb and trained him.[3] It remains to be witnessed any counter government efforts in Nigeria or even in the West to reduce the recruits of the youth who often are brainwashed by their recruiters and not sooner they were recruited sow seeds of hate, which would-be terrorists easily imbibe, putting their lives in danger and killing the innocent in the name of religion.

Therefore, for peace to reign and global security to be guaranteed (which incidents around the world show it may have made it more difficult to accomplish, world leaders have responsibilities to address that harmful phenomenon. While there are several dimensions to addressing the unending problems, one aspect of achieving peace and security could be support of true democracy in these affected regions that Jihadists have over–run fragile governments. Another method of taking the youths out of unemployment is by investments by developed countries in regions that Western investments (not donations or foreign aids) have not reached. Long neglects and disregard to economic development of poor performing countries around the world including African nations should be a matter of concern to the UN and world leaders. When our neighborhood in our global village is affected by poverty and underdevelopment, no matter how rich or well we may assume we are doing, the reality is that our self-worth and our society's wellbeing are affected by our neighbors' underdevelopment. It depreciates who we are as humans and as people and a nation when we assume poverty of our neighbor is not our business or does not affect us.

The IMF and the World Bank consist of non-governmental agencies positioned to address some of the economic problems facing developing countries because most of these countries, their leaders do not care about their people. It is in view of this observation that the leadership of these agencies that has been under the Western influence should also change. If the problems of the developing countries are to be addressed, it must be approached from the viewpoints of those that wear the shoes and know where it pinches most. Pundits believe that leadership from developing world that has experienced the problems these developing countries faced would be able to address these problems.

Similarly, they argue that developing countries are contributing almost 50% GDP and projected to contribute more than 60% GDP in 2030 to world economy.[6] With this in mind, they remarked there is need for shifts in leadership in IMF and World Bank organizations. Pundits disclose that it is not a must that a leader must be an African or from Africa or South America or Asia to be a good leader, however, these leaders coming from developing countries rather than every time from the US or Europe; leaders from developing countries may be in a better position to appreciate developing nations' problems and how to address them (since they have lived the problems and feel their pains). This may be the stepping-stone to resolving Africa's economic problems, pundits agreed.

As already witnessed since the 1960s, the "prescriptions" by these institutions to transform Africa has not yielded the desired economic results. Therefore, a new paradigmatic approach is required in the 21st century in appointing an African or a leader from a developing country should always be in charge to direct the affairs of these institutions that have been identified as determinants of financial flow and development around the world better. It is an argument that some disagreed, pointing out that Western or developed nations offering these leaders have performed better job of managing resources.

Finally, since poor countries with huge natural resources need the expertise and the resources of advanced economies to advertise and promote their resources in the global market, the role of UN agencies, such as the World Trade Organization, World Bank and IMF should be to assist these nations harness their terrorism is a network "business" not entirely about religion or ideologies as Jihadists have made us belief. This shifting paradigm of ideologies (business and religion) that international community must be concerned. It is urgent threat that needs attention to stop these insurgents wherever they emerged. Boko Haram declaring a captured Pulka village of Gwoza town in Maiduguri, Nigeria a Caliphate, barely two weeks after Islamic State of Iraq and Syria (ISIS) declared the areas it captured in Iraq and Syria Caliphate is not a mere coincidence. The ushering in "new era of international jihad" is a red flag to the global community that must not be taken for granted. It also revealed the suspected network between Boko Haram and its terrorist networks that has officially been limited to Al-Qaeda and Al-Shabaab. Al-Qaeda in Iraq and Syria were ordered immediately to pledge their allegiance to ISIS as soon as these cities in Iraq and Syria were captured and made a Caliphate.[7]

AFTERTHOUGHTS

Boko Haram, Terrorism and the Global Community

Despite the deployment of more than 2000 military men and women under the Joint Military Task Force to dislodge Boko Haram after Nigeria President Goodluck Jonathan declared State of Emergency in three Northern States of Adamawa, Borno and Yobe in North and Central Nigeria, Boko Haram has continued to unleash terror as the number of casualties continues to rise. The presence of international technical and security experts from United States, Britain, Canada, France, China, and Israel and to assist in the rescue efforts of the kidnapped Chibok schoolgirls has not slowed down the frequency of attacks and death tolls. Rather, Boko Haram has gained some territories; the Jihadists have also dislodged the National Police Mobile Training Camp in Limankara village of Gwoza Local Government Area of Borno state, while another group of terrorists, heavily armed stormed Pulka village of Gwoza and sacked the whole community. The Jihadists hoisted their black and white flags on August 21, 2014 declaring the town a Caliphate.[1] These incidents are taking place 120 days after the schoolgirls were abducted.

With two or more factions of Boko Haram terrorists operating in the North and Central States in Nigeria, there is confusion as to which of the groups is in charge of states they operate and the who is at the head of order and command in their hierarchy of leadership, and actually giving orders for attacks at any particular time. There have been claims and counter claims about responsibilities for various attacks previously linked to Boko Haram fighters, which leaders of the terrorist group has denied. As witnessed, a sect of the terror group claimed that it toppled Shekau recognized by Nigeria and the United States government as the leader of the terror group. It was later found out not to be true.

However, Mohammed who claimed he was the new leader of Boko Haram disclosed that he coordinated the simultaneous improvised bomb attack on Sabon Gari in Kano where 12 people died. The Joint Military Task Force had earlier announced that Abubakar Shekau was wounded following a raid to capture him. The claim appeared to be true as observers revealed that Abubakar Shekau appeared wounded and unstable as he appeared on YouTube video speaking about his triumph over the security agents after him. Also very clear was that whoever is in charge of the terror group or its factions, Boko Haram under Mohammed's command also conducted attacks on communities in the North and Central States. With Shekau declared a global terrorist by Washington, and placed a $7-million (5.3-million-euro) bounty for information leading to his whereabouts, the division witnessed within the terror group or the public claims of division even from factional group is not unexpected.

In August 12, 2003, Shekau's recognized as the original Boko Haram leader released a new video. On the video which he posted on YouTube, he claimed responsibility for the attacks in several Borno and Yobe communities including Malumfatori, Bama, Biu, Konduga, Gamboru Ngala, Gwoza, and Damaturu. About 100 people, among them 14 soldiers were killed in these attacks. In Konduga, on this August attack, 44 people were killed when gunmen dressed in military uniform opened gunfire on worshippers in a mosque.

Abubakar Shekau speaking in Hausa amidst his usual intermittent erratic 'victory' laughter said the military lied about its victories over Boko Haram. The video, received by AFP journalists showed Shekau refuting speculations that he was killed. "You have not killed Shekau," he ranted. "My soldiers were responsible for several deadly attacks in recent months," he claimed. Shekau – who leads the group's most deadly faction – boasted that his insurgents were stronger than the Nigerian military and that they were now strong enough to confront the United States. "I'm challenging Obama," Shekau said, issuing similar challenges to French President Francois Hollande and Israeli Prime Minister Benjamin Netanyahu. "They are no match for me."[2] He remarked that the Military was dishonest to the world about the confrontation the terrorists had with the Nigeria military. According to Shekau, the military is insincere about killing his members rather Boko Haram killed the soldiers. He remarked,

> "We call on you all to repent and come to the ways of Allah.
> Forget about constitution and accept Shariah. We don't have
> socialism, we don't know communism, we don't want federal
> ism, but we are Muslims……your soldiers have claimed that
> you are powerful, that we have been defeated, that we are
> mad people; but how can a mad man successfully coordinate
> recent attacks in Gamboru, in Malumfatori, slaughter people in
> Biu, kill in Gwoza and in Bama where soldiers fled under our
> heavy fire power."[3]

He further said that the group had killed countless soldiers and ready to kill more. "Our strength and firepower has surpassed that of Nigeria. Nigeria is no longer a big deal as far as we are concerned. We can now comfortably confront the United States of America," Shekau rumbly concluded.

"Let the world know that we have been enjoined by Allah to kill the unbelievers just like how we were enjoined to slaughter rams during Eidel Kabir. Moreover, we shall continue to kill those who strive to stand against the will of Allah by opposing Sharia. We don't mind if we die doing this because it is even a blessing for us to die in this cause and gain paradise. Therefore, we are winning on either side. So it is never too late for you to repent and join us on the path of right-eousness," he said.[4] The frequency of violence and huge number of casualties from Boko Haram attacks indicated the huge impact on lives of the people and the challenges it poses to the Joint Military Task Force to arrest the situation. With its objective to Islamize Nigeria, the Jihadists' declared "war" to make Nigeria a failed state, these efforts by terrorists to achieve their goal is unrelenting. It is the pattern of Al-Qaeda in Middle East and its Somalia-linked Al-Qaeda in the Islamic Maghreb.

Nigeria media and various international news sources in the United States and Europe played tremendously roles in the book you are reading. The details of information shared in this book revealing Boko Haram's outrageous assaults and suicide bombing would not have been detailed without the collaboration I received from Nigeria media. I have cited sources as I did here as authority to my credibility in bringing to the world details of menace by Boko Haram; the deadly harm the terrorists have caused to lives and families who have endured these attacks since 2009 when Boko Haram began its assaults on Nige-rians and foreign workers. Without media information to the public, especially the Nigeria media that is less appreciated than they deserved, the list compiled here would not have been possible. Thanks to colleagues in the media, that have compile and forward to me references through the Internet when I was inundated by the frequency these stories on Boko Haram's attacks occurred. I also wish to express deep appreciation to several academic and non-academic authors that I have used. You provided me the opportunity to compare my list with what you have and update as I tallied the data you read now.

President Barack Obama highlighted the problems Boko Haram and other terror networks posed to the security of the global village. President Bush's also warned during his war on terrorism post 9/11 about the imminent danger posed to global security. With terrorist now taunting Nigeria, the country should not be left not alone or isolation in dealing with the problems of terrorism even after Chibok schoolgirls were eventually rescued. As President Obama also highlighted in Soweto during a town- hall meeting with young Africans including youth leaders from Nigeria who joined the conference through satellite, "Terrorism is bound to exist in countries that have neglected or failed to take care of their people." He further disclosed leaders in respective countries where terrorists operate should unite and collaborate with international community to fight the terrorism. On the victims of most terrorist attacks, the president revealed that majority of the victims in all terror attacks are citizens of the country where the terrorists operate. A majority of more than 12,000 victims of Boko Harams terrorism were Nigerians. The same could be said of victims of terror in Iraq, Pakistan and Afghanistan. . The rhetoric is often "The West is the target of terror, but the majority of the victims are not Westerners," the president said.

The bombing of the US Embassies in Kenya and Tanzania was the first of terror attack in Africa that were masterminded by Al-Qaeda in the Islamic Maghreb (AQIM). Investigations to the attacks led to the Al-Qaeda involvement in the planning of the attacks. It also led to FBI declaration of Osama Bin Laden as the Most Wanted Person on its list of criminals around the World. In these attacks, Africans were majority victims even though Western institutions were targeted. Investigations later revealed that Al Qaeda undoubtedly carried out the bombing in response to American involvement in the extradition and alleged torture of four Egyptian Islamic Jihad (EIJ) members arrested in Albania two months before the explosion in Kenya and Tanzania took place. As was the simultaneous patterns of bombing – the trade mark of Al Qaeda, the bombings of the U.S. Embassies in Nairobi and Dar es Salaam killed 224, including 212 Africans, 12 Americans, and injured more than 5,000.[5]

On the solution to the problem of fundamentalism and terrorism, there is no doubt that the military option or the use of force may not be the only solution to address the problem. It has more to do with the attitude of leaders, political and religious who exploit the weakness of the human mind and motivate the vulnerable weak to be motivated to beliefs espoused by religious or political bigots, most of the time for their (leaders') selfish interests.

After examination of the suicide bombing that is used to "send" a message about the ideologies these radicals advocate, there is no single incident in all the suicide bombings or military-style attacks that these politicians and clerics in Iraq, Afghanistan, Pakistan, Indonesia, Philippines, Somalia, Nigeria or elsewhere have ever used their sons or daughters to fight and promote their so-called Jihadists' agenda. Sending other children to die for the causes they espoused indicates that something is wrong, somewhere. The solution to dislodging terrorists therefore takes the commitment of every citizen to fight the war. It entails vigilance; it entails ensuring that the so-called religious leaders and politicians that finance some of these groups must be exposed. Similarly, clerics that promote radicalism or extreme form of Islam that they have hijacked from the majority of good Muslims must be made to understand that they are wrong and in the minority. Counties promoting terrorism as a form of opposition army or proxy political groups must be isolated.

Finally, the statement by President Obama, that terror cannot be eradicated by military force resonates here. Evidence of US and Allied Forces war on terror in Iraq and Afghanistan and in 2014, several years after the war that cost billions of dollars, the terrorists persist show how military power does not and will not win the war on terror. Indeed, the world should isolate regimes that treat their people as if they don't matter or important.

The huge capital flight siphoned through corruption and capital flight has new countries that accept such ill-gotten wealth. Europe, and the United States used to be the destinations, but countries in the Middle East, Qatar and Dubai are alleged new locations of money laundry for corrupt politicians and officials. Terrorists' main sources of income remain individuals' contributions, robbery of banks and ransoms paid for the release of kidnapped victims; however, the use of banks for money transfer remains terrorists' means of moving large sums of money across borders.

When terror happens, it affects us all no matter how far we may think we are far from the location of these deadly assaults. In the age of Internet Communication Technology (ICT), distance is no longer a barrier as witnessed with several events in recent times that happened thousands of miles, but were able to influence our lives as well as our responses. It is not about "us" and "them" and vice versa when it is about terrorists and what they can do. Terrorists' attacks do not discriminate or distinguish "us" and "them" as long as we are perceived as infidels, no matter the color of our skin, our economic status and our residence.

On the economic drive that may lead some to criminal behaviors including participation in insurgence or terrorism; a hungry man is indeed an angry man; we can reduce the motivation by politicians and clerics to young and unemployed youths to join their Jihad by stopping the lure by fundamentalists (religious and political leaders) from using their wealth and religion to lure or brainwash the weak and the poor to violence in the name of martyrdom. When the world becomes a place, where the majority of the youth is employed and has no reasons to depend on the clerics or politicians that drive their motivation to terrorism may be the intervention will see less of youth being recruited by fundamentalists. Violence, no doubt could be minimized by creating jobs and wealth. Like terrorism and racism, these are like life's problems to be lived with, but we can reduce their consequences and agree to solve them – now and in the future to save lives. It is an obligation we must fulfil as individuals and nations in a global village.

All May Come to Pass...But at What Costs?

Nigerians, in particular Muslim leaders from the North must move very swiftly to find solution to the security challenges confronting the country. With Boko Haram terrorists' attacks, Nigeria is perceived under attack around the world, not Northern or North Central Nigeria as often framed in political dialogue in the country. There have been too much talk and less action about how to get the real faces behind Boko Haram's violence. Northern politicians seemed to be hands off, leaving the Federal Government to find solutions to the insecurity in these Northern States of Maiduguri, Yobe and Adamawa.

Knowing that Nigeria and Northern parts of the country is a collectivistic society where vigilante and neighbors look after others property and lives, it beats the imagination that the Northern leaders allowed Boko Haram to grow to monster that is uncontrollable. However, if the Northern leaders are serious and wanted to tell the world that they are ready to stop the killings by Boko Haram, it is high time they unmask Boko Haram members or their leaders. Now is the time to call the Jihadists throwing bombs and grenades, and causing mayhem all over the region to order. Now is the time to summon an emergency meeting of the emirs and other traditional rulers in the region to identify who were members of Boko Haram and bring them to order.

Since the dialogue over offer of amnesty was botched stopping terrorists' deadly assaults – including sacking villagers and mounting their flag of authority in the name of declaring Caliphate must be stopped. In Africa, when a community rises against any uprising, such insurgence always failed. That model of African life - it takes a village should be embraced to fight terrorism and terrorists. This means that no matter how sophisticated the equipment of terrorists is, the will and power of the armed communities will defeat them. Let truth be told, if the region is on the boil, it is clearly a failure of leadership (in the region) and Nigeria. It is not every time we blame others for our woes. As citizens, we should take responsibility by identifying infiltrators among us, whose objective it is to destroy what they did not build. We also must look inwards, and take a slice of the knocks if we do nothing individually by providing intelligence and making other contributions to stop terrorists. If we all are determined and honest about the grave issue about terrorism, its impact on lives of people and Nigeria economy, I am hopeful that not all hope is lost as we seek to navigate out of the Boko Haram quagmire. What Boko-Haram is doing under the guise of a religion is not something anybody could ever understand. It should not be tolerated and certainly adds no value to any culture or religion and society in general.

Acknowledgements

As a journalist myself, I never appreciated the work reporters do until I began to read thousands of pages of stories and news articles on issues on the headline news like Boko Haram terrorists and the kidnapped Chibok schoolgirls. Knowing that journalist provide news on this and other matter of importance and significance everyday becomes more awakening – just as the talents and the sacrifices these men and women exhibit everyday to provide knowledge that impact all of us and the decision leaders make to improve the world. I personally congratulate journalists, editors, publishers, producers, cameramen and women (others behind the scene that hardly are seen by the viewer or readers of the news) who provide us the news circle 24/7 and 365 days every year without any disruptions (even by the conflicts and wars they cover and some do lose their lives in the process. In spite of media shortcomings, the enormous work journalists do to inform the world about events as they happen around the world need to be appreciated and I do so here.

Special thanks friends and colleagues in the media. My deep appreciation goes particularly to Nigeria national media, the international news media, newspapers, magazine and televisions, bloggers in Nigeria – online and off line dailies that I followed every day to read and understand the deadly attacks, kidnappings and suicide bombing incidents, details that some are contained here. The list are long but for space here are some of the news media organizations - *The Van guard, the Sun, the Punch,   ThisDay, the Guardian, Leadership, the Nation, Premium Times, and the Naija Pundit, the Africa Spotlight,* CKN.com, Naij.com, *and Xclusive* Magazine. Please if your organization is not listed here, it is an oversight and not a deliberate act of omission.

On the list of international media in the US and around the world, British Broadcasting Corporation (BBC), Aljazeera News Network, Africa, CNN (international), Associated Press, French News Agency (AF), News Agency of Nigeria, Sahara reporters.com, AllAfrica.com, bloggers too numerous to mention here; Human Rights Watch, Wikipaedia.org.

There is no way I could have followed and captured all the events without the media stories and news about these incidents as they occurred. Boko Haram also publicized its activities through its website. I did use some of their releases including ones posted online.

Thanks to my colleagues in the media that forwarded some of the references as Boko Haram's attacks (assaults) occurred in the news. If your organizations name is missed in this acknowledgement, please note that it is not deliberate act. Thank you all.

I decided to go the length in citing, and sometimes paraphrasing quotes and interviews I used the sources in this book to ensure that the International community that most times under rate and see the Nigeria and the Africa's problems from the perspectives of the Western media and international Press understand an enormous intelligent investigative journalism and reporting African journalist do. I also provided tried to provide unadulterated viewpoints by people journalists interviewed of issues of national and international security from multi cultural perspectives of the reporters and interviewees.

Thanks again to men and women of the fourth estate of the realm – without you the world will turn into anarchy. Your audacity to face and challenge status quo and defend the public from the butchery of elite club milking the people to death and terrorists like Al-Qaeda and Boko Haram threatening the fabric of societies and what we believed have worked and do not need the extremists or Stone Age anarchic ideologies to change.

I owe this book project to my editors who worked tediously under tight deadline with me and eventually brought the writing to what you are reading. Thank you for your patience and understanding.

NOTES

1. President Barak Obama speaking at White House following the kidnapping of more than 300 Chibok Schoolgirls – of which 53 later escaped from the captors. Also available via facebook. Retrieved May 15, 2014 from https://www. facebook. com/White House?hc_location=timeline.

2. CNN (Abuja, Nigeria) (2014, May 5). Boko Haram attacks Nigerian village used by military in search for abducted girls. Retrieved May 15, 2014 from http://www.cnn.com/ 2014/05/ 07/world/africa/nigeria-abducted-girls/. See also Fox News (May 8, 2014) Boko Haram attacks Nigerian village used by military in search for abducted girls. http://fox4kc.com/2014/05/08/boko-haram-attacks-nigerian-village-used-by-military-in-search-for-abducted-girls/.

3. U.S. Secretary of State, Senator John Keerey making official statement after Boko Haram reported kidnapping of Chibok Schoolgirls from Government Secondary School Chibok, Maiduguri, Nigeria. See also New York Times (May 3, 2014). 'Bring Back Our Girls'. Retrieved May 5, 2014 from http://www.nytimes.com/ 2014/05/04/ opinion/sunday/kristof-bring-back-our-girls.html?_r=0

4. Malala Yousafzai, Taliban shooting victim and Pakistani education activist was in Abuja on her 17th birthday to mark three months since Boko Haram abducted 276 girls from a secondary school in Chibok, in the northeast. See AFP (July 14, 2014). Malala tells Nigeria president to meet parents of hostages. Retrieved July 14, 2014 http://africvilla.com index.php /africa2/10-nigeria/2508-malala-tells-nigeria-president-to-meet-parents-of-hostages#sthash..ZpymwiFI.dpuf.

PROLOGUE
APRIL

1. *Guardian* (2014, May 5). Missing Nigerian schoolgirls: Boko Haram claims responsibility for kidnapping - Islamist militants' leader threatens to sell the more than 270 girls abducted in northeast Nigeria on 14 April. Retrieved May 10, 2014 from http://www.theguardian.com/ world/2014/may/05/boko-haram-claims-responsibility-kidnapping-nigeria-schoolgirls.

2. *New York Post* (2015, March 13). ISIS accepts Boko Haram's pledge of allegiance. Retrieved March 14, 2015 from http://nypost.com/2015/03/13/isis-accepts-boko-harams-pledge-of-allegiance. See also *Voice of America* (VOA) News. (2015, March 11) Nigeria's President: Boko Haram Trained with Islamic State. Retrieved March14, 2015 from http://www.voanews.com/content/nigerias-president-says-boko-haram-trained-with-islamic-state/267 6217.html.

3. *Punc*h (2014, May 5). CAN releases names of 180 abducted schoolgirls. Retrieved May 10, 2014 from http://www.punchng.com/news/can-releases-names-of-180-abducted-schoolgirls/

4. *ThisDay* (2014, May 30). Boko Haram Kills Emir of Gwoza in Highway Ambush. Retrieved June 1, 2014 from http://www.thisdaylive.com/articles/boko-haram-kills-emir-of-gwoza-in-highway-ambush/179815/.

5. *New Telegraph (2014, July 7)*. 65 women, girls escape from Boko Haram in Borno. Retrieved August 3, 2014 from http://newtelegraphonline.com/65-women-girls-escape-from-boko-haram-in-borno/

6. Africvilla.com (2012, May 5). Funding of Terror Network: 'Boko Haram got over N11bn to kill and maim.' Retrieved May 8 2014 from http://africvilla.com/index.php/africa2/10-nigeria/2094-funding-of-terror-network-boko-haram-got-over-n11bn-to-kill-and maim#sthash.CmuASV69.See also Security agents arrest 8 foreigners. Punch (May 4, 2014). Retrieved from http://www.punchng.com/ newssecurity-agents-arrest-8-foreigners/.

7. Associate Press (2014, July 14). Boko Haram leader demands fighters' release for schoolgirls; claims attacks, 1st Lagos bombing. Retrieved July 15, 2014 from http://www.foxnews.com/world/2014/07/14/boko-haram-leader-demands-fighters-release-for-schoolgirls-claims-attacks-1st/. See also Tele-graph(July14,2014)http://www.telegraph.co.uk/news/worldnews/africaandindianocean/nigeria/10964606/Missing-Nigerian-schoolgirls-Boko-Haram-issues-new-video-mocking-BringBackOurGirls-campaign.ht

8. *New York Times* (2014, May 7). Abduction of Girls an Act Not Even Al Qaeda Can Condone. Retrieved June 12, 2014 from http://www.nytimes.com/2014/05/08/world/africa/ abduction-of-girls-an-act-not-even-al-qaeda-can-condone.html?_r=0

9. IMF (April 2014). Nigeria: 2013 Article IV Consultations, Staff Report, Press Release & Statement by the Executive Director of Nigeria. IMF Country Report No. 4/103. Retrieved April 22, 2014 from http://www.imf. org/external/pubs/ft/scr/2014/cr14103.pdf. See also http: //www.imf.org/external/country/ NGA/index.htm.

10. Associated Press (2014, May 10). First lady gives weekly address on Nigerian girls. Retrieved May 10, 2014 from http://news.yahoo.com/first-lady-gives-weekly-address-nigerian-girls-101142983.html.

11. Ibid.

CHAPTER 1
BOKO HARAM - WHY THE NEW TACTICS OF TERRORISM [THE KIDNAPPING OF CHIBOK SCHOOLGIRLS]

1. Foucault, M. (1985). The History of Sexuality, Volume 2: The Use of Pleasure. United States: Random House.

2. CNN (2014, May 5, 2014). I will sell them,' Boko Haram leader says of kidnapped Nigerian girls. Retrieved June 16, 2014 fromhttp://fox4kc.com/2014/05/08/boko-haram-attacks-nigerian-village-used-by-military-in-search-for-abducted-girls/.

3. Ibid.

4. See also Foucault, M. (1986) The History of Sexuality, Volume 3: The Care of the Self. United States: Random House. Foucault, M. (1978). The History of Sexuality, Volume 1: An Introduction.United States: Random.

5. *The Punch* (2014, June 12). I have access to Boko Haram, says Obasanjo.RetrievedJune18,2014fromhttp://www.punch ng.com /news/i-have-access-to-boko-haram-says-obasanjo.

6. Mirror.co.uk (2014, August 16). Islamic State fanatics kidnap more than 3,000 women and girls in 2 week rampage. RetrievedAugust27, 2014fromhttp://www.mirror.co.uk/news/ world-news/islamic-state-fanatics-kidnap-more-4062810#ixzz3BbyWvwXn.

7. http://rt.com news (August 15, 2015). ISIS militants massacre 80 Yazidis, kidnap women in Iraqi village. Retrieved August 27, 2014 from http://rt.com/news/ 180712-isis-massacre-village-iraq/. See also The Guardian (2014, August 11). Yazidis tormented by fears for women and girls kidnapped by Isis jihadists.RetrievedAugust27, 2014 fromhttp://www.theguardian. com/world/2014/aug/11/yazidis-tormented-fears-for-women-girls-kidnapped-sinjar-isis-slaves

8. The Guardian (2014, June 26). Up to 186 Kurdish students kidnapped by Isis in northern Syria. Retrieved August 27, 2014 from http://www.theguardian. com/world/2014/jun /26/186-kurdish-students-kidnapped-isis-syria

9. *CNN with Christine Amanpour* (2014, May 6). Nigeria's government acting like children, says Nobel-winning author Wole Soyinka.RetrievedMay8, 2014fromhttp://amanpour.blogs. cnn.com/2014/05/06/nigerias-government-acting-like-children-says-nobel-winning-author-wole-soyinka/.

CHAPTER 2

NOT WITH OUR DAUGHTERS – BOKO HA-RAM & THE KIDNAPPING OF 300 CHIBOK SCHOOLGIRLS: A PATTERN OF TERROR THE WORLD MUST UNITE AND STOP

1. BBC News (2014, April 21) Chibok abductions in Nigeria: 'More than 230 seized. Retrieved April 30, 2014 from http://www.bbc.com/news/world-africa-27101714.

2. Eribon, Didier (1991) [1989]. Michel Foucault. Betsy Wing (translator). Cambridge, MA: Harvard University Press.

3. France 24, International News (2012, February 24). Boko Haram has links to al Qaeda, Nigeria's military chief says. Retrieved October 10, 2013 from http://www.france24.com/en/20120223-nigeria-boko-haram-al-qaeda-islamist-militant/

4. Vanguard Newspaper (2013, April 3). Boko Haram Tactics Baffling _ Army Chief Alerts the Press. Retrieved April 3, 2013 from http://www.vanguardngr.com /2013/04/boko-harams-tactics-baffling-ihejirika/

5. Associated Press (2013, March 15). Head of US Africa command warns of Islamic threat. Retrieved June 10, 2013 from http://www.houstonchronicle.com/ news/politics/ article/Head-of-US-Africa-command-warns-of-Islamic-threat- 4357815.php.

6. *Vanguard* (2014, March 9). Al-Qaeda takes over Boko Haram. Retrieved May 5, 2014 from http://www.vanguardngr.com/ 2014/03/al-qaeda-takes-boko-haram/

7. The Nation (2014, August 25). Boko Haram: Row over 'desertion' of 480 soldiers. Retrieved August 27, 2014 from

http://thenationonlineng.net/new/boko-haram-row-over-desertion-of-480-soldiers/

8. ABC News.Com (2012, May 6, 2014). Home: International 'Bring Back Our Girls' Becomes Rallying Cry for Kidnapped Nigerian Schoolgirls. Retrieved May 6, 2014 from http://abcnews.go.com/International/ bring-back-girls-rallying-cry-kidnapped-nigerian-schoolgirls/story?id=23611012. See also http://www.change.org/petitions/over-200-girls-are-missing-in-nigeria-so-why-doesn-t-anybody-care-34girls/suggested _petitions. See also

9. *Leadership* (2013, March 21). Nigeria: Kano Multiple Blasts - There's a Grand Design to Set Nigeria On Fire – Sultan. Retrieved October 10, 2013 from http://allafrica .com/stories/201303210215.html. See also Leadership (July 30, 2013). Kano Multiple Explosions Ungodly-Sultan. http://leadership.ng/news /300713/kano-multiple-explosions-ungodly-sultan/.

10. *HelloBeautiful.com* (2014, April 30). Kidnapped Nigerian School Girl Escapes Terrorist-group. Retrieved May 1, 2014 from http://hellobeautiful.com/2014/04/30/ kidnapped - nigerian-school-girl-escapes-terrorist-group-said-nothing-will-happen-to-you/?omcamp=EMC-CVNL.

11. Ibid

12. CNN (May 3, 2014). Nigerian police: 223 kidnapped girls still missing. Retrieved May 3, 2014 from http://www.cnn.com/2014/05/02/world/africa/nigeria-abducted-girls/.

13. Omoregie, H. (2014, April 29). The Sons of Sardauna. *ThisDay* Retrieved April 30, 2014 from http://www. Thisday live.com/articles/the-sons-of-sardauna/177270/.

14. BBC News Africa (June 4, 2013). United States offer rewards for capture of African militants. Retrieved July 20, 2013f romhttp://www.bbc .co.uk/ news/world-africa- 22763305.See also AFP (June 3, 2013 at http://www.vanguardngr.com/ 2013/06/united -states-places-23-million-reward-for-shekur-4-others.

15. Amnesty International (2014, March 30). Nigeria: War crimes and crimes against humanity as violence escalate in North East. Retrieved April 12, 2014 from http://www.amnesty. ca/news/ news-releases/nigeria-war-crimes-and-crimes-against-humanity-as-violence-escalates-in-north. See also Vanguard (2014, March 26). 1,000 killed in Boko Haram conflict this year – NEMA. Retrieved April 12, 2014 from http://www. vanguardngr.com/2014/03/1000-killed-boko-haram-conflict-year-nema/#sthash.hxoo5niR.dpuf.

16. Omoregie, H., ThisDay (2014, April 29). The Sons of Sardauna. Retrieved April 30, 2014 from http://www.thisdaylive .com/articles/the-sons-of-sardauna/177270/.

17. Daily Trust (2012, May 4). What Boko Haram Fighters Told Me About Sect? - Governor Kashim Shettima. Retrieved May 6, 2014 from http://saharareporters.com/ interview/ dailytrust-interview-what-boko-haram-fighters-told-me-about-sect-governor-kashim-shettima.

18. Vanguard (2014, April 26). Ex-Ghanaian President warns FG on Boko Haram says insurgency may persist unless....Retrieved May 1, 2014 from http://www.vanguardngr.com/2014/04/ex-ghanaian-president-warns-fg-boko-haram-says-insurgency-may-persist-unless/#sthash.BXTnASZy.dpuf. See also Africvilla.com (2014, April 28, 2014) Military alone cannot stop insurgency in Nigeria – Rawlings. Retrieved from http://africvilla.com/ index./africa2/2050-military-alone-cannot-stop-insurgency-in-nigeria-rawlings#sthash.0dpC4v2K.voE2STXj.dpuf.

19. Ibid

20. The Punch (2012, April 26). Time to make a choice. Retrieved May 2, 2014 from http://www.punchng.com/opinion/ letters/ time-to-make-a-choice.

21. Ibid

22. Mayer, J. (2008). The Dark Side: The Inside Story of How The War on Terror Turned into a War on American Ideals. Double-day. New York, NY. See also Al Qaeda operative key to 1998 U.S. Embassy bombings killed in Somali. Retrieved July 10, 2012 from http://articles. latimes.com/2011/jun/12/world/la-fg-embassy-bombings-20110612

CHAPTER 3

BOKO HARAM – IN THE BEGINNING

1. *Punch* (2011, November 30). Al-Qaida wants to kidnap westerners in Nigeria. Retrieved June 15, 2013 from

   http://www.punchng.com/index.php?option=com_k2&view=item&id=6188:al-qaeda-wants-to-kidnap-westerners-in-nigeria-%E2%80%93-report&Itemid=542. Algeria is also home to the AL Qaida in the Islamic Maghreb. The group identified by security agencies (European, US and African) as providing both logistics and training to the violent Islamic sect in the Northeast of Africa.

2. *The Nation* (2014, August 25). Boko Haram: Row over 'desertion' of 480 soldiers. Retrieved August 28, 2014 from http://thenationonlineng.net/new/boko-haram-row-over-desertion-of-480-soldiers/

3. *Premium Times* (2014 May 17). Boko Haram Has Killed Over 12,000 Nigerians, Plans To Take Over Country, Jonathan Says. Retrieved May 20, 2014 from http:// saharareporters.com/ news-page/boko-haram-has-killed- over- 12000-nigerians-plans-take-over-country-jonathan-says-premium-t.

4. *African Spotlight* (2013, April 20). Boko Haram Freed French Hostages Recount their ordeal. Family members of French citizens were kidnapped in Cameroon on February 19, 2013; taken

to neighboring Nigeria and on Thursday, April 18, they were handed over to Cameroonian authorities. See Also AfricanSpotloight.com (April 26, 2013). Boko Haram was paid N500 million before freeing French hostages – report. Retrieved August 4, 2013 from http://www.africanspotlight.com/tag/ french-hostages/

5. Johnson, Toni (2013, August 31). "Backgrounder: Boko Haram". Council on Foreign Relations. Retrieved 2011- 09-01. Retrieved April 13, 2013 from http://www.cfr.org/africa/boko-haram/p25739.

6. Vanguard (2013, April 10). Boko Haram amnesty: You are on suicide mission, Christians tell FG. Retrieved April 11, 2013 from http://www.vanguardngr.com /2013/04/boko-haram-amnesty-youre-on-suicide-mission-Christians-tell-fg.

7. CNN (2013, February 15). Attackers kill 3 North Korean physicians in Nigeria, official says. See also U.S. State Department Human Rights Report on Nigeria (2013). United States Department of State (2013). Bureau of Democracy, Human Rights and Labor Country Reports on Human Rights Practices for 2012. Retrieved November 21, 2013 from http://www.state.gov /j/drl/rls/hrrpt/human right sreport/index.htm?year =2012&dlid=204153.

8. Reuters (2012, January 9) "Islamist sect has support in Nigerian gov't: president." In September 2012, however, the military announced that they had arrested an immigration official and some security personnel alleged to have links to Boko Haram attacks in Borno and Yobe states. See "Nigerian security officers arrested for Boko Haram links,"

9. Vanguard (2012, January 9). Pres. Jonathan's bombshell - "Boko Haram members are in my Government!" Retrieved May 6, 2013 from http://www.vanguardngr. com/Pres-Jonathan's-bombshell- Boko- Haram-members- are –in- my-Government

10. Ibid

11. Ibid

12. AFP, September 29, 2012. The Nigerian authorities filed criminal charges in November 2011 against a senator from Borno State, Ali Ndume, for alleged links with the group, an allegation Boko Haram denied. See section below, Prosecution of Boko Haram Suspects. In February 2012, the authorities dismissed a police commissioner, Zakari Biu, for his alleged role in the escape from police custody of Kabiru Sokoto, the alleged mastermind of the Christmas Day 2011 bombing in Madalla. Vanguard (2012, February 27). Secretly Reinstated, Publicly Dis-missed. Retrieved March 26, 2013 from http://www.vang uardngr.com /2012/02/zakari-biu-secretly-reinstated-publicly-dismissed/

13. Punch (2013, April 3). Govt blasts Buhari for comment on insecurity. Retrieved March 26, 2013 from http://www.punchng.com/news/govt-blasts-buhari-for-comment-on-insecurity/

14. Vanguard Newspaper (2013, April 3). Boko Haram Tactics Baffling _ Army Chief Alerts the Press. Retrieved April 3, 2013 from http://www.vanguardngr.com /2013/04/boko-harams-tactics-baffling-ihejirika/

15. Associated Press (2013, March 15). Head of US Africa command warns of Islamic threat. Retrieved June 10, 2013 from http://www.houstonchronicle.com/ news/politics/ article/Head-of-US-Africa-command-warns-of-Islamic-threat- 4357815.php.

16. Ibid

17. Boko Haram-Ansaru: We have killed 7 kidnapped captives. Retrieved March 17, 2013 from http://naijagists.com/boko-haram- ansaru-weve-killed-7-kidnapped- french-captives/.

18. Vanguard (2013, May 20). Rev. Jesse Jackson Backs Amnesty for Boko Haram. Retrieved, May 26, 2013. From http://www.vanguardngr.com /2013/05/ rev-jesse-jackson-backs- amnesty-for-boko-haram/

19. Ibid

20. Olusegun Obasanjo's second coming having ruled Nigeria before as a military head of state between 1976 and 1979.

21. BBC (2014, June 6). More Nigerian girls abducted by suspected Boko Haram militants. Retrieved June 10, 2014 from http://www.bbc.com/news/world-africa-27298614

22. American.Aljazeera.Com (2014, August 15). Boko Haram abducts nearly 100 boys and men during village raid. Retrieved August 28, 2014 from http://america.aljazeera.com/articles/2014/8/15/bokoharam-nigeriaabduction.html

23. Reuters (2014, June 8). Female suicide bomber hits Nigerian barracks: witnesses. Retrieved June 9, 2014 from http://news.yahoo.com/blast-kills-least-three-outside-nigerian-barracks-witnesses-144938127.html.

24. Black Lloyd, D. (1967). US Economic Aid to Africa. *African Studies Bulletin* Vol. VII, No. 1. March.

25. Susanne Rice (2005, June 27). US Foreign Assistance to Africa: Claims vs. Reality. Brookings Institute. Retrieved March 18, 2013 from http://www.brookings. edu/articles/2005/0627 africa_rice.aspx.

CHAPTER 4

BOKO HARAM: THE REAL FINANCIERS - CASH FLOW AND ITS GLOBAL TERROR NETWORKS

1. Lyman, Princeton N. & Morrison, J. Stephen (2004). The Terrorist Threat in Africa. Foreign Affairs, January/February, 2004. Also online at http://www.foreign affairs.com/ articles/59534/princeton-n-lyman-and-j-stephen-morrison/ the-terrorist-threat-in-africa. See also Jane Mayer, *The Bomb Dark Side*, Doubleday. See also Al Qaeda operative key to 1998 U.S. Embassy bombings killed in Somali. http://articles.Latimes .com /2011/jun/12/world/la-fg-embassy-bombings-20110612.

2. *AFP,* Washington (2013, June 3). U.S. Places $23 million Reward for Boko Haram Leaders, Shekau, 4 others. Re-

trieved June 30, 2013from http://vanguardngr.com /2013/ 06/ united-statesplaces-23m-reward-for-shekau-4-others/

3. Al-Arabiya News (2014, July 13). Boko Haram voices support for ISIS' Baghdadi. Retrieved July 17, 2014 from http://english.alarabiya.net/en/News/africa/ 2014/07/13/Boko-Haram-voices-support-for-ISIS-Baghdadi.html.

4. *The Nation* (2012, January 29). Tracking the Sect's Cash Flow. Retrieved June 29, 2013 from http:// www. thenation-non lineng.net/tracking-the-sect's-cash-flow/.

5. *SundayTrust* (July 7, 2013). JTF Detains Borno ANPP Chairman. Retrieved August 12, 2013 form http://sundaytrust. com.ng/index php/top-stories/ 13636-jtf-detains-borno-anpp-chairman.

6. Ibid

7. Ibid

8. Ibid

9. Ibid

10. Ibid

11. Ibid

12. *SundayTrust* (2013, July 7). JTF Detains Borno ANPP Chairman. Retrieved August 3, 2013 from http://sundaytrust.com.ng/index.php/top-stories/13636-jtf-detains-borno-anpp-chairman.

13. *Tribune* (2013, February 13). Boko Haram's Funding Traced to UK, Saudi Arabia-Sect Planned to Turn Nigeria into Afghanistan.

14. Africvilla.com (2014, May 4). Funding of Terror Network: 'Boko Haram got over N11bn to kill and maim. Retrieved May5, 2014from http://africvilla. com/index.php/africa2/10-

nigeria/2094-funding-of-terror-network-boko-haram-got-over-n11bn-to-kill-and-maim#sthash.CmuASV69.dpbs.

15. AllAfrica.Com (2012, February 14). Boko Haram's Funding Sources Uncovered. Retrieved June 28, 2013 from http://allafrica.com/stories/201202141 514.html

16. *Tribune* (2012, May 21). Boko Haram's Funding – Nigeria May Face International Sanctions. Retrieved March 19, 2013 from http://dailypost.com.ng/2012 /05/21/boko-haram-funding-nigeria-may-face-international-sanctions.

17. *Premium Times* (2014, May 12). Chibok Schoolgirls: Israel offers counter-terrorism experts for rescue mission. Retrieved July 6, 2014 from http://www. premiumtimesng.com/news/160555-chibok-schoolgirls-israel-offers-counter-terrorism-experts-rescue-mission.html.

CHAPTER 5

BOKO HARAM – EXPLOITING THE ART OF PROPAGANDA & MEDIA PUBLICITY

1. Boko Haram leader, Abubakar Shekau Message. You-Tube Video (2012, January 12) Retrieved September 12, 2012 from http://saharareporters.com/video/video-boko-haram-leader-imam-abubakar-shekau-message- President Jonathan.

2. *ThisDay* (2010, December 27). Jos Bombings –Group Claims Responsibility. Retrieved September 10, 2012 from http://allafrica.com/stories/201012280 145.html.

3. *Leadership* (2012, April 9). Easter Bombing - Bodies Were Lying Everywhere – Survivors. Retrieved on April 9, 2012 from http://allafrica.com/stories/201204090157.html.

4. *Vanguard* (2013, February 14). Nigeria: Boko Haram – Cease – Fire or Ceaseless Fire. Retrieved February 20, 2013 from http://allafrica.com/stories /20130216108/html. See also Sahara Reporters. (April 8, 2013). Dancing With Ghosts, Ignoring the Dead.

5. Human Rights Watch, October 2012. See also Imam Imam and Seriki Adinoyi, "Jos Bombings - Group Claims Responsibility," ThisDay (Lagos), December 27, 2010, http://www.thisdaylive.com/articles/jos-bombings-group-claims-responsibility/71232/).

6.   Ibid

7. Human Rights Watch interviews with Christians in Maiduguri, Maiduguri, July 2010. See Human Rights Watch Report, October 2012.

8. Ibid.

9. Human Rights Watch Report (October 2012). Spiraling Violence.

10. Ibid.

11. *Sun News* (2013, May 26) Femi Fani-Kayode: The Woolwich killing and the Illuminati - More questions than answers - Some things just don't add. Retrieved May 27, 2013 from http://www.sunnewsonline.net/ news/femi-fanikay.

12. Ibid.

13. This is a part of conspiracy theory disseminating in colleges and universities and it was used to motivate students to be science rather than majoring in arts and social sciences.

14. *Vanguard* (2013, April 3). Boko Haram insurgency, a conspiracy? (1). Retrieved May 26, 2013 from http://www. vanguardngr.com/2013/04/boko-haram-insurgency-a-conspiracy-1/

15. Ibid.

CHAPTER 6

BOKO HARM TERROR ATTACKS – WHY THE IGBOS (SOUTH EASTERN CHRISTIANS) ARE EASY TARGETS OF FUNDAMENTALISTS IN NIGERIA

1. Lyman, Princeton N. & Morrison, J. Stephen (2004). The Terrorist Threat in Africa. Foreign Affairs, January/February, 2004. Also online at http://www.foreign affairs.com/articles/59534/princeton-n-lyman-and-j-stephen-morrison/ the-terrorist-threat-in-africa.

2. *The Daily Trust* (April 3, 2013). Agree on amnesty for Boko Haram and I'll lead negotiations - Former governor of Abia State, Orji Uzor Kalu. http://dailytrust .com.ng/index.php/politics/ 53813-agree-on-amnesty-for-boko-haram-and-i-ll-lead-negotiations. Orji-Kalu suggested that Igbos suffer most by President Jonathan refusing to grant amnesty to Boko Haram.

3. *AFP* (August 24, 2013). Thousands of Nigerian Muslims protest to demand return of Egypt's ousted President. http://www.africanspotlight .com/2013/08/24/thousands- of-nigerian-muslims-protest-to-demand- return-of-egypt's-ousted-president/. Retrieved August 26, 2013.

4. *Associated Press* (February 19, 2013). French family of 7 kidnapped in Cameroon, including 4 children. http://www.foxnews.com/world/ 2013/02/19/7-french-citizens-kidnapped-in-cameroon-official-The five French family members were kidnapped in border town of Nigeria and Cameroon as chips for exchange of Boko Haram members arrested and detained by the Federal agencies in Nigeria.

5. *The Sun* (April 20, 2013). Kalu tables issue of Igbo marginalization before British parliament. On line

http://sunnewsonline.com/new/cover /kalu-tables-issue-of-igbo-marginalization-before- british-parliament/ Retrieved on April 23, 2013).

6. J.W.C. Pennington (1841). *A textbook on the Origins and History of the Colored People* (Hartford, CT: L. Skinner), 96.

7. Tudor Parfitt (2013). Black Jews in Africa and the Americas. Harvard University Press, Cambridge, Massachusetts, MA. 107.

8. George, T. Bardin (1921). *Among the Igbos of Nigeria: An Account of the Curious and Interesting Habits, Customs and Beliefs of a Little Known African People, by One Who has Many Years Lived Among Them on Close & Intimate Terms.* (London: Seeley, Service & Co. 1938[1st ed. 1921]), 31-32.

9. Isichei, Elizabeth (1976). *A History of the Igbo People*. London, England: Macmillan.

10. [66] Olaudah Equiano (1789). The Interesting Narrative of the Life of Olaudah Equino or Gustavus the African.

11. Tudor Parfitt (2013). Black Jews in Africa and the Americas. Harvard University Press, Cambridge, Massachusetts, MA.

12. Blum. Jeffrey, D (1969, February 25). Who Cares About Biafra Anyway? Retrieved February 8, 2014 from http://www.thecrimson.com/article/1969/2/25/ Who-cares-about-biafra-anyway-pithis/#.UvZKeb8r Gew.facebook

13. Igbo Jews – Shavei Israel – For our Lost Brethren. Retrieved August 12, 2013 from http://www.shavei.org/categories/ communities. See also Re - emerging: The Jews of Nigeria. A Documentary Film by Jeff L. Lieberman. www.re.emergingfilm.com.

CHAPTER 7

BOKO HARAM – NEGOTIATING AMNESTY AMIDST SPIRALING VIOLENCE & DEATHS.

1. Human Rights Report (October, 2012). Spiraling Violence.
2. Ibid.

3.   Ibid.

4.   *Vanguard* (November 25, 2011). We are on a revenge mission,
     Boko Haram suspect tells the court. Retrieved September 10,
     2012 from http://www.vanguardngr. Com/2011/11/we-are-on-
     revenge-mission-boko-haram-suspect-tells-court.

5.   *This Day* (September 22, 2010). Boko Haram claims killings in
     Borno. Retrieved September 30 from http://www.thiddaylive
     /article/boko-haram-claims-killing-in-borno/78273.

6.   Human Rights Watch Report, October 2012.

7.   Human Rights Watch Report, October 2012. Sahara Report-
     ers.com (May 22, 2013). Some Nigerian Soldiers Help Boko
     Haram – Lt. General Ihejirika. Retrieved July 30, 2013 from
     http://saharareporters.com /news-page/some-nigerian-soldiers-
     help-boko-haram-lt-general/.

8.   Human Rights Watch Report, October 2012.

     The NaijaPundit.com (August 2, 2013). Coup in Boko Haram
     as Shekau is Toppled by His Lieutenants. Retrieved, August 3,
     2013 from http://www.naija pundit.com/ news/coup-in-boko-
     haram-as-Shekau-is-toppled-by-his's-lieutenants/

9.   Human Rights Report – *Spiraling Violence*.

     October, 2012.

10. Ibid 19. See also Congressional Testimony by Assistant Secre-
     tary Johnnie Carson, US Department of State, House Foreign
     Affairs Committee, Subcommittee on African Affairs, "U.S.
     Policy Towards Nigeria: West Africa's Troubled Titan," July
     10, 2012.

11. Ibid

12. Ibid

13. AP (2014 April 14). Blast rips up busy bus station in Nigerian capital. Retrieved April 14, 2014 from http://news.yahoo.com/blast-rips-busy-bus-station-nigerian-capital-082718610.html. See similar story on Saharareporters.com on http://saharareporters.com/ news-page/abuja-bus-station-bombing-update

14. CNN (2014, February 20) Diplomatic talks in Ukraine last until dawn, a day after 100 may have died. Retrieved April 2, 2014 from http://www.cnn.com/2014/02/20/world/europe/ukraine-protests/

15. *The Nation* (May 16, 2013). Nigeria continued violence worries UN Chief. Retrieved June 10, 2013 from http://www.thenationonlineeng.net/ news-update/nigeria-continue-violence-worries-un-chief/.

16. *Punch* (February 27, 2013). Poverty fuelling Boko Haram insurgency – Clinton. Retrieved June 20, 2013 from http://www.punchng.com/news/ poverty-fuelling-boko-haram-insurgency-clinton/

CHAPTER 8

OPINIONS ON GRANTING AMNESTY TO BOKO HARAM - VIEWS FROM EMINENT POLITICIANS, TRADITIONAL AND RELIGIOUS LEADERS.

1. *Vanguard* (March 16, 2013). Boko Haram: Mixed reactions trail call for Amnesty. Retrieved April 4, 2013 from http://www.vanguardngr.com/2013/03/boko-haram-mixed-reactions-trail-call-for- amnesty/

2. *The Leadership* (2013, March 31). Matthew Hassan Kukah-Easter Message: Amnesty, Repentance, Forgiveness and

Reconciliation.Retrieved April 4, 2013from http://leadership.ng/nga/articles/51192/2013/03/31/easter_ message_amnesty_repentance_forgiveness_and _reconciliation. html.

3. Ibid.

4. From Amnesty to Repentance |. (2013, March 31). Retrieved April 4, 2013 from http://aworship.com/from-amnesty-to-repentance/

5. *Vanguard* (April 3, 2013). Boko Haram should repent, apologize before amnesty – Onaiyekan. Retrieved April 4, 2013 from http://www.vanguardngr.com/2013/04/boko-haram-should-repent-apologise-before-amnesty-onaiyekan/.

6. Information Nigeria (April 1, 2013). Amnesty Call: Sultan Is Encouraging and Condoning Bloody Violence – Afenifere. Retrieved April 4, 2013 http://www.information ng.com/2013/03/amnesty-call-sultan-is-encouraging-and-condoning-bloody-violence-afenifere.html.

7. News Agency of Nigeria (NAN) (March 31, 2013). Amnesty For Boko Haram: Sultan Goofed – CAN. Retrieved April 30, 2013 from http://www.informationng.com /2013/03/ amnesty-for-boko-haram-sultan-goofed-can.html.

8. *Vanguard* (April 3, 2013). Anglican Bishop to Boko Haram: Unmask before seeking amnesty. Retrieved April 11, 2013 from http://www.vanguardngr.com/2013/04/anglican-bishop-to-boko-haram-unmask-before-seeking-amnesty/

9. *Vanguard* (April 10, 2013). Boko Haram amnesty: You're on suicide mission, Christians tell FG. Retrieved April 11, 2013 from http://www.vang uardngr.com/2013/04/boko-haram-amnesty-you're-on-suicide-mission-christians-tell-fg/.

10. Ibid.

11. *Punch* (March 31, 2013) If I Was President, I Would Grant Amnesty to Boko Haram-Atiku. http://www.naijapundit .com/news/if-i-was-president-i-would-grant-amnesty-to-boko-haram-atiku.

12. Ibid.

13. *Vanguard* (March 31, 2013). President's Easter Message to Nigerians. See also Boko Haram are not Muslims (March 31, 2013). President Good luck Jonathan speaking in his Easter Holiday message to Nigerians. Retrieved April 11, 2013 from http://naijamayor.com/boko-haram-are-not-muslims-goodluck-jonathan/? fb_source=pubv1.

14. *Naija Pundit* (April 11, 2013). After Establishing Drone Base in Niger U.S. Now Says Boko Haram Insurgency will soon end. Retrieved April 11, 2013 from http://www.naijapundit.com/news/ after-establishing-drone-base-in-niger-u-s-now-says-boko-haram-insurgency-will-soon-end.

15. *The Leadership* (April 9, 2013). Nigeria: Northern Elders to Govs - Bring Boko Haram Members for Dialogue.
Retrieved April 11, 2013 from http://allafrica.com/stories/01304100195.html? page=2.

16. *Vanguard* (May 19, 2013). Rev. Jesse Jackson Backs Amnesty for Boko Haram. Retrieved May 26, 2013 from http://www.vanguardngr.com/2013/05/rev-jesse-jackson-backs-amnesty-for-boko-haram/.

17. *The Nation* (May 26, 2013). Boko Haram: US secretary of state Kerry meets Jonathan. Retrieved May 27, 2013 from http://thenationonlineng.net /new/news-update/boko-haram-us-secretary-of-state-kerry-meets-jonathan/.

18. Ibid

19. *Daily Trust* (April 3, 2013). Agree on amnesty for Boko Haram and I'll lead negotiations - Former governor of Abia State, Orji Uzor Kalu. Retrieved June 18, 2013
From http://dailytrust.com.ng/index.php/politics/53813-agree-on-amnesty-for-boko-haram-and-i-ll-lead-negotiations.

20. Ibid.

21. Information Nigeria (April 2, 2013). Boko Haram Begins Mass Recruitment. Retrieved May 12, 2013 from http://www.informationng.com/2013/04/boko-haram-begin-mass-recruitment.html.

22. Ibid.

23. Vanguard (April 4, 2013). Boko Haram is your baby, Buhari fires back at Jonathan. Retrieved April 5, 2013 from http://www.vanguardngr.com/2013/04/boko-haram-is-your-baby-buhari-fires-back-at-jonathan/.

24. Ibid.

25. Ibid.

26. African Spotlight (April 6, 2013). Jonathan, forgive Boko Haram Retrieved April 7, 2013 from Turai.http://africanspotlight.com/2013/04/jonathan-forgive-boko-haram-turai/

27. Ibid.

28. *Naija* (April 7, 2013). PDP, CAN, ACF Disagree On Amnesty For Boko Haram. Retrieved April 6, 2013 from http://news.naij.com/ 30126.html.

29. Ibid

30. Ibid

31. Ibid

32. *Vanguard* (April 21, 2013). Boko Haram Amnesty: Scratching the surface of a nation's festering sore. Retrieved April 24, 2013 from http://www.vanguardngr.com /2013/04/boko-haram-amnesty-scratching-the-surface-of-a-nations-festering- sore/.

33. *Vanguard* (April 8, 2013). We're yet to decide on amnesty – Boko Haram. Retrieved April 8, 2013 from

http://www.vanguardngr.com/2013/04/we-re-yet-to-decide-on-amnesty-boko- haram/.

34. *Naija Pundit* (April 8, 2013). Boko Haram to FG We Reject Your Amnesty! Retrieved April 9, 2013 from http://www.naija   pundit.com/news/boko-haram-to-fg-we-reject-your-amnesty.

35. *Vanguard* (April 10, 2013). Boko Haram amnesty: You're on suicide mission, Christians tell FG. Retrieved April 11, 2013 from http://www.vanguardngr.com/2013/04/boko-haram-amnesty-youre-on-suicide-mission-christians-tell-fg/

36. AFP (July 30, 2013). Nigeria bombs kill 24 in mainly Christian area. http://au.news.yahoo.com/world/a/-/world/18234403/nigeria-bombs-kill-24-in-mainly-christian-area/ . Retrieved August 5, 2013. See also Vanguard (August 5, 2013). 35 Killed as Boko Haram, JTF Clash. http://www.vanguardngr.com/2013/08/35- killed-as-boko-haram-jtf-clash/.

37. *Vanguard* (August 2, 2013). Turaki – Journalists at War of Words Over Boko Haram Peace Committee's Findings). Retrieved, August 5, 2013 from http://www.vanguard ngr.com/2013/08/turaki-journalist-at-war-of-words -over-boko-haram-peace-committee's-finding.

38. Saharareporters.com (2013, August 3). There is Grand Design to Plunger Northern Nigeria into Deeper Crisis – Sultan. Retrieved August 3, 2013 from http://saharareporters .com/ news-page/there-grand-design-plunge-northern-nigeria-deeper-crises-sultan. See also There Is a Grand Design to Plunge Northern Nigeria Into ... (2013, August 3). http://www.nigeriasun.com/index.php/ sid/216165307/scat/8db1f72cde37faf3

CHAPTER 9

NIGERIA – SHADING THE IMAGE OF A FAILED STATE

1. *Vanguard* (April 12, 2013). Nigeria is a terrorist state – Gen Idada. Online at http://www.vanguardngr.com/2013/04/nigeria-is-a-terrorist-state-gen-idada/. Retrieved April 15, 2013

2. Ibid.

3. Ibid.

4. Pope Francis begs Boko Haram to free hostages (March 31, 2013) Retrieved April 5, 2013 from .http://www.xclusive nigeria.com/index.php/component/k2/item/492-pope-francis-begs-boko-haram-to-free-hostages.

5. Boko Haram are not Muslims (March 31, 2013). President Good luck Jonathan speaking in his Easter Holiday Message to

Nigerians. Retrieved April 5, 2013 from http://naijamayor .com/boko-haram-are-not-muslims-goodluck-jonathan/?fb_source=pubv1.

6. *Sahara Reporters* (April 8, 2013). Give Boko Haram Amnesty, Save Nigeria From War and Military Intervention – Muslim Group. Retrieved April 14, 2013 from http://sahara report-ers.com/news-page/give-boko-haram-amnesty-save-nigeria-war- and-military-intervention- 93-muslim-group

7. *Xclusive Magazine* (April 8, 2013). Nigerians too timid for revolution – Amaechi. Retrieved April 12, 2013 from http://www.xclusivenigeria. com/index php/news-stories.

CHAPTER 10

TERRORISM & SECTARIAN VIOLENCE - A REFLECTION ON NIGERIA' S PAST, PRESENT & WAYS FORWARD

1. Lyman, Princeton N. & Morrison, J. Stephen (2004). The Ter-rorist Threat in Africa. *Foreign Affairs*, January/February, 2004. Retrieved May 9, 2013 from http://www.foreign **af-**fairs.com/articles/59534/princeton-n-lyman-and-j-stephen-morrison/ the-terrorist-threat-in-africa.

2. Ibid

3. Allen, J.L. (2013). The Catholic Church: What Everyone Needs to Know? Oxford University Press. New York. Associated Press (2012, February 17). "Underwear bomber Umar Farouk Abdul Mutallab sentenced to life in prison". Daily Mail (Lon-don). Retrieved August 18, 2013 from http://www. dai-lymail.co.uk/news/article-2102254/ Underwear-bomber-Umar-Farouk -Abdulmutallab-sentenced-life-prison.html.

4. *New York Times* (June 11, 2003). Ugandan's Key to White House: AIDS.

5. *This Day* (April 6, 2012). 51 Rocket Launchers uncov-ered in Gombe. Retrieved April 10, 2012 from http://allafrica.com /stories/ 201204060768.html.

6. *The Organization for Economic Co-operation and Development* (OECD) (2010). Perspectives on global development Economy: Developing countries set to account for nearly 60% of world GDP by 2030, according to new estimates. Retrieved March 17, 2015 from http://www.oecd.org/dev/pgd/economy developingcountriessettoaccountfornearly60ofworldgdpby 2030 accordingtonewestimates.htm.

7. *The Independent* (2014, August 26). Iraq crisis: Isis declares its territories a new Islamic state with 'restoration of caliphate' in Middle East. Retrieved August 26, 2014 from http://www.independent. co. uk/ news/world/ middle-east/isis-declares-new-islamic-state-in-middle-east-with-abu-bakr-albaghdadi-as-emir-removing-iraq-and-syria-from-its-name-9571374.html

AFTERTHOUGHTS
BOKO HARAM, TERRORISM & THE GLOBAL COMMUNITY.

1. The Independent (2014, August 26). Iraq crisis: Isis declares its territories a new Islamic state with 'restoration of caliphate' in Middle East. Retrieved August 26, 2014 from http://www.independent. co. uk/ news/world/ middle-east/isis-declares-new-islamic-state-in-middle-east-with-abu-bakr-albaghdadi-as-emir-removing-iraq-and-syria-from-its-name-9571374.html

2. Africanspotlight.com (August 13, 2013). No match for me': Boko Haram leader challenges Obama, two other foreign powers in new video. Retrieved August 14, 2013 from http://www.africanspotlight. Com/2013/08/13/no-match-for-me-boko-haram-leader-challenges-obama-2-other-foreign-powers-in-new-video/.

3. Saharareporters.com (August 13, 2013). Boko Haram Leader Pokes Fun At US, France, Claims Sect Winning War Against Nigerian Military-PREMIUM TIMES. Retrieved August 14, 2013 from http://saharareporters. Com/news-page/boko-haram-leader-pokes-fun-

us-france-claims-sect-winning-war-against-nigerian-military-premium time.

4. Ibid

5. See Jane Mayer, The Bomb Dark Side, Doubleday. See also Al Qaeda operative, key to 1998 U.S. Embassy bombings killed in Somali. Retrieved June 18, 2013 from http://articles.latimes. com/2011/jun/12/ world/la-fg-embassy-bombings-20110612

www.ingramcontent.com/pod-product-compliance
Lightning Source LLC
Chambersburg PA
CBHW060246290526
45789CB00001B/210